Introduction

Marriage is a disaster area in America. Over one million divorces have taken place every year in the United States since 1975. In many of our major cities one out of every two marriages ends in divorce.

Many married couples never received good premarital counseling, since marriage did not look very complex to them when they were engaged. But after years of bumps, struggles, tears, and emotional hurts, marriage seems much more difficult, and counseling is often needed.

We delight in counseling couples who have a respect and commitment to God's Word as authoritative in their lives. This makes solutions to their problems much easier, for we believe that harmony and happiness can be restored if both parties are truly willing to yield to the Lord and to the guidance of His Word.

The statistics are much more encouraging here. Only one out of forty marriages of those who regularly attend church ends in divorce. And only one out of four hundred marriages ends in divorce when the couple reads the Bible and prays together. These statistics are significant—Christian homes that honor God's Word and follow His teaching have a greater potential for success.

We have counseled hundreds of married couples with a wide variety of socioeconomic, racial, cultural, and religious backgrounds. From our extensive experience (as pastor, and as psychiatrist and seminary professor), and from the research studies we have examined, we have concluded that there are certain vital factors *essential* for a spiritually and emotionally healthy home. The seven elements we consider crucial are: (1) a spiritual base; (2) genuine love; (3) gut-level communication; (4) discipline; (5) consistency; (6) setting the example; and (7) proper leadership roles.

The chapters that follow cover these major areas in which most family problems are likely to occur. This guidebook is not designed to take the place of personal counseling, but it may help to give positive direction. By discussing family foundations from a biblical perspective, we hope to aid families in recognizing and avoiding the difficulties that have a way of threatening the stability of the Christian home.

Paul Meier, M.D.
Rev. Richard Meier

For further information regarding the nationwide services of the Minirth Meier New Life Clinic, please call
1-800-NEW-LIFE (Clinical Services) or
1-800-266-5745 (National Resources Division)

Seven Secrets
for a Happy
Family

Books authored or co-authored by Paul Meier
Happiness Is a Choice
Introduction to Psychology and Counseling
Christian Child-Rearing and Personality Development

Books authored or co-authored by Richard Meier
Sex in the Christian Marriage
The Healthy Christian Life
Husbands and Wives
Filling the Holes in Our Souls
What They Didn't Teach You in Seminary
The Passages of Life Bible

Seven Secrets for a Happy Family

Paul Meier and Richard Meier

© 1981 by Paul Meier and Richard Meier

Published by Fleming H. Revell
a division of Baker Book House Company
P.O. Box 6287, Grand Rapids, MI 49516-6287

Spire edition published 1997

Third printing, October 1997

Previously published by Baker Book House under the title *Family Foundations: How to Have a Happy Home*

Printed in the United States of America

ISBN 0-8007-8642-4

For current information about all releases from Baker Book House, visit our web site:

http://www.bakerbooks.com

Contents

One

A Spiritual Base

We believe that all humans have three basic needs—a sense of self-worth, intimacy with others, and intimacy with God. All three of these are acknowledged in the great commandment, summarized by Jesus Christ in Mark 12:29-31. Christ said, "The foremost is, '. . . You shall love the Lord your God with all your heart, and with all your soul, and with all your mind, and with all your strength.' The second is this, 'You shall love your neighbor as yourself.' There is no other commandment greater than these" (NASB). The Bible indicates that all the other laws of Scripture hang on this great commandment, and that if we obey this one, we necessarily obey all the other commandments. Love God; love your neighbor; love yourself. (We must note that genuine self-love is the opposite of false pride, which is a sin committed by those trying to compensate for their feelings of self-loathing.)

Without a vital personal relationship with Jesus Christ, however, no human has the power within himself to consistently meet his three basic needs. As counselors we often hear patients use the word *can't*. They say, for example, "I just can't get along with my husband." "My husband and I can't communicate." "I can't seem to discipline my children the way I should." I can't give up the affair I am having." "I can't find a job." "I can't stop overeating." "I can't love my wife—I've tried."

When a non-Christian uses the word *can't*, we believe him. A non-Christian, without the power of God in his life, really cannot choose righteous paths consistently. But for a Christian, "I can't" and "I've tried" are merely lame excuses. The Bible tells Christians in Philippians 4:13, "I can do all things through Christ who strengthens me." In I Corinthians 10:13, Christians are told that God will never allow them to be tempted beyond their strength, but will provide a way (and the power) to escape sinful temptation.

We insist that our Christian patients be honest with themselves and use language that expresses the reality of the situation. We have our patients change their *can'ts* to *won'ts*: "I just won't get along with my husband." "My husband and I just will not communicate." "I will not discipline my children the way I should." "I won't give up the affair I'm having." "I will not find a job." "I won't stop overeating." "I won't love my wife—I'll make a half-hearted effort at loving her but I won't quite succeed." If an individual changes all his *can'ts* to *won'ts*, he stops avoiding the truth, quits deceiving himself, and starts living in reality.

The Christian who continually fails is defeating himself; he is his own worst enemy. The Christian who is depressed is depressed because he is choosing (either out of ignorance of the Word or else purposely) to be depressed. He is choosing not to live by God's principles. God wants him to see the fruit of the Spirit in his life, and that fruit includes love (not pent-up anger or bitterness), joy (not depression), and peace (not anxiety—see Gal. 5:22, 23). Whoever does not have the fruit of the Spirit is not living by the Spirit.

Of course, Christians are not without problems; they have conflicts just like everyone else. However, they do have an excellent resource to draw upon to solve those problems. But before Christ can be seen as a resource to help solve depression, an individual must first accept Christ as his Savior.

To accept Christ, or believe in Christ, means basically two things. First, the individual must know certain facts. For example, he must know that Christ was more than just a good man. He is also the Son of God. He died on a cross for the sins of the world. He made payment in full for the sins of whoever would turn to Him. Not only did He die on the cross for our sins, but He also arose from the grave and was victorious over death. These are the basic facts about Christ which must be known by the individual. However, merely knowing these facts is not enough. Second, the individual must have a personal relationship with Christ. He must believe in Christ.

Belief in Christ starts with a choice of the will. The degree of the emotional conviction involved in the choice will differ from individual to individual. We have counseled quite a few people who were afraid they did not believe enough. They seemed to be confusing belief with full emotional persuasion. We explained that belief in-

volves the will, while emotions are sometimes evasive and
hard to change. They may be rooted in psychological
problems of many years past. For example, a woman who
had been unable to trust or depend on her parents may
have trouble feeling that she can always trust and depend
on God. Belief for her must begin with the will; later, as
she spends time growing in Christ and in His Word, her
emotions will change and she will find emotional re-
assurance as well.

It is interesting to note that in the Gospels alone the
word *believe* (or its equivalent) is listed 115 times as the
condition for salvation. In this connection consider the
following verses from the New Testament:

> But as many as received him, to them gave he power to
> become the sons of God, even to them that believe on his
> name (John 1:12).

> For God so loved the world, that he gave his only begotten
> Son, that whosoever believeth in him should not perish,
> but have everlasting life (John 3:16).

> And [the Philippian jailer] brought them [Paul and Silas]
> out, and said, Sirs, what must I do to be saved? And they
> said, Believe on the Lord Jesus Christ, and thou shalt be
> saved, and thy house (Acts 16:30, 31).

> For the wages of sin is death; but the gift of God is eternal
> life through Jesus Christ our Lord (Rom. 6:23).

> For whosoever shall call upon the name of the Lord shall
> be saved (Rom. 10:13).

> For by grace are ye saved through faith; and that not of
> yourselves: it is the gift of God: Not of works, lest any man
> should boast (Eph. 2:8, 9).

To believe is simply to rely on Christ and what He has done for us, accepting His death on the cross in our place for the punishment of our sins. Belief is realizing that Christ died for our sins, and trusting in Him to save us. Trusting Christ is a matter of the will. God does all the work, through Christ's atonement and the Holy Spirit's conviction—we humans merely choose to accept salvation or we choose to reject it. Note that there is no third alternative. To be passive about salvation is the same as choosing to reject it. And according to John 3:16-18 and scores of other passages, judgment awaits those who actively or passively reject Jesus Christ as Savior.

Once an individual accepts Christ, he has available to him a tremendous resource that he did not have before, since God becomes his personal father. As most earthly fathers desire to help their children, God much more desires to help His children when they suffer in any way.

Next in importance to having Christ in one's heart is the practice of Christ's principles in one's home. Below are some basic, practical helps for extending your spiritual base from your heart to your home.

First, we must regard human beings holistically, as a complex interweaving of body, soul, and spirit. Thus if we feed a child well and use healthy psychological principles, but ignore his spiritual development, we will be developing only two-thirds of a person. I believe the development of the child's spirit is the most important of the three. Psychological development will enable a child to live in society and earn a living, but spiritual development will enable him or her to understand the meaning of life. Carl Jung once stated, "The least of things with a meaning is worth more in life than the greatest of things without it." This observation has been borne out in my own practice, for some of my patients have had everything this world can offer and yet they were groping desperately to find meaning.

One of the most exciting experiences in a Christian's life is to assist a young child to accept Christ as Savior. This is especially true if his parents have lovingly guided his spiritual development by following God's commandments to teach (Deut. 6:6, 7), to train (Prov. 22:6), and to bring up (Eph. 6:4) their child in a way that would enable him to experience the abundant life (John 10:10). This is where Christian men have fallen short. They have become so wrapped up in their work that they have neglected their highest calling—the spiritual development of their children.

God tells us fathers that

> He established a testimony in Jacob,
> And appointed a law in Israel,
> Which He commanded our fathers,
> That they should teach them to their children;
> That the generation to come might know, even the
>   children yet to be born,
> That they may arise and tell them to their children,
> That they should put their confidence in God,
> And not forget the works of God,
> But keep His commandments (Ps. 78:5, 7, NASB).

God has also said,

> And these words, which I command thee this day, shall be
> in thine heart: And thou shalt teach them diligently unto

thy children, and shalt talk of them when thou sittest in thine house, and when thou walkest by the way, and when thou liest down, and when thou risest up (Deut. 6:6, 7).

God gave instruction to "know well the condition of your flocks, and pay attention to your herds" (Prov. 27:23, NASB). Solomon told us that "in the fear of the Lord there is strong confidence, and his children will have refuge" (Prov. 14:26, NASB). These verses reveal our tremendous responsibility before God to encourage spiritual development in our children. Let's discuss ways to do this in each age group.

Prenatal

Obviously, a pregnant woman cannot teach her child Bible verses before he is born. She can, however, help to make his prenatal environment as beneficial as possible by enjoying the pregnancy, listening to soothing music, and taking good care of her physical, emotional, and spiritual needs. Many scientists believe that such measures can positively influence the developing baby. Maternal attitude can affect the rate of miscarriages as well as the rate of congenital abnormalities.[1]

Infant (birth to fifteen months)

Some of the foundations for spiritual development are laid during infancy. Though the infant certainly does not understand doctrine or theology, he will be affected by a

1. Virginia Hight Laubaran, and Bea J. Van den Berg, *American Journal of Obstetrics and Gynecology* (February, 1980), p. 46.

family's religious beliefs. Such concepts strongly influence the attitudes parents have toward the infant. He or she can sense the overall home atmosphere, and will begin to respond to parental behavior and attitudes.

Toddler (fifteen to thirty-six months)

At this stage the child rapidly acquires language skills, grasps for new experiences, and observes everything that happens in his small world. How the toddler and his father relate to each other is extremely influential in the child's concept of God. A parent must realize that though he can teach his toddler to say a memorized prayer to a loving, heavenly Father, the child's perspective of God will depend on what his earthly father is like. If a child's own father is harsh and critical, his conception of the Father to whom he is praying will be negatively influenced. But if the child is in a loving, secure, and accepting environment during these months, he will develop a basic trust that will enable him later to have a meaningful faith in God. What parents allow their child to watch on television, the kind of music they play, and the tone of voice they use in the home strongly influence the child's personality development. These factors will either facilitate or hinder his future spiritual development.

Preschooler (three to six years)

During these years, a child adds thousands of words to his vocabulary, but his knowledge of abstract concepts is still almost nil. He reasons concretely, and everything is either black or white. This is known as *dichotomous* thinking. Without a stimulating environment and some formal education, a child may never outgrow this dichotomous approach to experience. To preschoolers, words are just that—words. Gary Collins mentions that even during the national anthem, young children frequently substitute words like "the grandpas we watched were so gallantly screaming."[2] They also often misunderstand the words in hymns. Such errors may be humorous to adults, but they indicate how children reason at this age.

The Swiss psychologist Jean Piaget did extensive research on the neurological, social, and moral development of children.[3] He even set up a behavioral timetable for the child's earlier years. From his studies, we know (among other things) when the average child will say his first word, be neurologically ready for toilet-training, understand concrete concepts, tie his shoes, and understand abstract concepts. Piaget's studies show that three- to six-year-old children reason quite literally, and they believe almost all that parents tell them. The average child, in a relatively good school system, doesn't begin to reason ab-

2. Gary Collins, *Man in Transition: The Psychology of Human Development* (Carol Stream, Illinois: Creation House, 1971).
3. See the following works by Jean Piaget: *The Moral Judgment of the Child* (Glencoe, Illinois: The Free Press, 1948); *The Origins of Intelligence in Children* (New York: International Universities Press, 1952); *The Construction of Reality in the Child* (New York: Basic Books, 1954); *Logic and Psychology* (New York: Basic Books, 1957); *The Language and Thought of the Child* (New York: Humanities Press, 1959); *Play, Dreams and Imitation in Childhood* (New York: Norton, 1962); *The Mechanisms of Perception* (New York: Basic Books, 1969).

stractly until he is about eleven years old.[4] That is why attempts to reason with a three- to six-year-old child about his misconduct are frequently a waste of time. A quick spanking to bring repentance is much more effective and useful in dealing with children this age. They can understand that if they do certain bad things, the result will be either a short verbal rebuke or else quick physical punishment; and if they do certain good things, the result will be parental praise, approval, and maybe even a big hug.

Parents need to understand the child's level of reasoning in order to effectively teach him spiritual things. For example, stories about Jesus and some of the children in the Bible mean a great deal to a child at this age, whereas abstract teaching about, say, parable interpretation or "agape" love will only make him wish his parent would hurry up so he can get back to his toys. The more appropriate the spiritual training the child has during these three years, the more he will rely on his Christian faith when he is older. We believe some children at age four through six can understand enough to know that they are frequently sinful, that they want God to forgive them, and that they want to live forever in heaven. They are old enough to put their faith in Christ; indeed, Christ taught that unless an adult puts faith in Him "like a little child," he will not inherit the kingdom.

As parents help their three- to six-year-olds develop spiritually, they must keep in mind that parental words are not the main sources of the children's learning. At

4. John Peters, "Lectures on Piaget," at the University of Arkansas Child Study Center, Little Rock, Arkansas, July, 1973.

church or at home, it is the child's total life experiences that count. As Gary Collins says, "A 'loving heavenly Father' is foolishness if the child's earthly father is harsh and unkind. . . . Even the child's views of God, Heaven, angels, and Hell are in terms of pictures he has seen."[5] Children this age frequently pray as though God were a magician in the sky whose purpose is to grant their wishes. (A great number of adults still pray in this thoughtless and selfish way. They try to use God's "magic" to accomplish their will, instead of asking God to show them *His* will.) As we pray with our children, we should show them by our example that prayer is a means of merging our will with the will of God. During this stage of development, children pick up their notions of right and wrong from what they see us doing, not from what we say is right or wrong.

Over four hundred years ago, Michelangelo wrote, "The more the marble wastes, the more the sculpture grows." This statement also applies to the psychological and spiritual development of our children. Approximately 85 percent of the adult personality is already formed by the time a child reaches his sixth birthday. After the sixth birthday, a parent's primary task is to chip away at the last 15 percent of marble in an attempt to sculpt his child into a Christian young adult.

During those twelve years from the sixth to the eighteenth birthdays, a lot of psychological and spiritual struggles can take place in the family—and many of them are totally unnecessary. The best way to make it easy on our-

5. Collins, *Man in Transition*, p. 53.

selves as parents during this twelve-year period is to love and discipline our children effectively during those crucial first six years of life. As King Solomon wrote under the inspiration of God nearly three thousand years ago, "Train up a child in the way he should go: and when he is old, he will not depart from it" (Prov. 22:6). By age eighteen, a son or daughter should be ready to move out of the house, just as a young robin is ready to face life on its own when its mother pushes it out of the nest. Parents must trust their offspring's God-given ability to make his or her way in the world "on his own two wings."

Elementary school age

Identification

Most children are quite cooperative during the elementary school years. They want to please their parents and teachers and adopt the morals of their parents. They continue to identify with the parent of the same sex, learning both his good and bad habits. Healthy and unhealthy communications between the parents themselves greatly affect the child's own sense of self-worth.[6] A father who is criti-

6. James F. Alexander, "Defensive and Supportive Communications in Normal and Deviant Families," *Journal of Consulting Clinical Psychology* 40 (April 1973):223-31; Haim G. Ginott, *Between Parent and Child* (New York: Avon Books, 1965); Sigfrid R. McPherson, et al., "Who Listens? Who Communicates? How? Styles of Interaction Among Parents and Their Disturbed Adolescent Children," *Archives of General Psychiatry* 28 (March 1973):393-99; Linda Odom, Julius Seeman, and J. R. Newbrough, "A Study of Family Communication Patterns and Personality Integration in Children," *Child Psychiatry and Human Development* 1 (Summer 1971):272-85; Kent Ravenscroft, Jr. "Normal Family

cal of his wife is also unknowingly tearing down the self-confidence of his daughters; the same applies to mothers who criticize their husbands.

The budding conscience

The conscience continues to grow during these years. And, because he has a model to copy, the identification with the parent of the same sex strengthens the child's self-control. He continues to reason concretely until about the age of eleven, when, if properly educated, he can begin to reason out abstract concepts.[7]

The total devotional atmosphere

We would encourage parents to create a total devotional atmosphere in their home. By this we do not mean the family sitting in a corner praying all day. We mean loving, communicating, playing with the children, and exhibiting the fruit of the Spirit. One way to enhance the devotional atmosphere is to have some good sacred music on from time to time, geared to the age of the children. This should not be to the exclusion of good secular music, for we cannot separate our lives into secular and sacred. Every part of our lives is sacred—even going to the baseball game and eating hot dogs!

Having family devotions together is extremely impor-

Regression at Adolescence," *American Journal of Psychiatry* 131 (January 1974):31-35; G. Rice, J. G. Kepecs, and I. Yahalom. "Differences in Communicative Impact Between Mothers of Psychotic and Nonpsychotic Children," *American Journal of Orthopsychiatry* 36 (September 1971):363-77.

7. Peters, "Lectures on Piaget."

tant. These should be quite brief for children in this age group, or devotions will become a torture to endure rather than a happy time of sharing Christ with each other. Mealtimes are excellent times for family devotions, but parents should be creative. One idea is to have the child give a short "book report" on a Christian story he has read. Or, he can recite a Bible verse he has memorized (such verses should, of course, be short and understandable to a child).

But let us emphasize that the spiritual tone in the home is not set solely by a time of family prayer or Bible reading. Children absorb the total home environment, and will be far more likely to center their lives on Christ if the Lord's loving care is acknowledged in every life situation.

Church environment

The church you take your family to is even more important. We would refer you to the writings of Gene Getz for what we consider a psychologically and spiritually sound church.[8] A healthy church can be one of the best influences in the emotional and spiritual development of children. The kind of church we mean stands on three legs, like a tripod: (1) a sound doctrinal leg; (2) an evangelistic leg; and (3) a relational leg, with genuine sharing and intimate love among the members of that local body of believers.[9]

8. Gene A. Getz. *The Christian Home in a Changing World* (Chicago: Moody Press, 1972); *Sharpening the Focus of the Church* (Chicago: Moody Press, 1974); *The Measure of a Church* (Glendale, California: Gospel Light, 1975).
9. These concepts about a healthy church are discussed in Gene Getz's excellent book, *Sharpening the Focus of the Church.*

Outside influences

Christian camps are a good outside influence on the spiritual development of children. I worked at Pine Cove Camp in Tyler, Texas, one summer while I was still in medical school. It was a marvelous experience. Pine Cove has the philosophy that if you wear a child out all day by letting him have some good old-fashioned fun, then he will listen to a brief but strong gospel message late in the evening around a campfire. That was really effective. Hundreds come to know Christ each summer and many more rededicate their lives to the Lord. There is probably a similar camp near you—ask your pastor.

Right and wrong

Hartshorne and May have conducted a series of experiments on the moral development of children.[10] Their experiments reveal that though children learn more about right and wrong as they grow older, they become increasingly deceptive. Hartshorne and May found that children who were honest in certain situations were dishonest in others. Children with lower intelligence, emotional instability, or from lower socioeconomic environments also lagged behind in moral development. One of the most significant findings was that children who were enrolled in Sunday schools showed significantly better conduct in the areas of honesty, cooperation, persistence, and inhibition of undesirable behavior.[11]

10. H. Hartshorne and M. A. May, "A Summary of the Work of the Character Education Inquiry."
11. Ibid.

Moral development

Jean Piaget's studies of moral development in children show that moral behavior is learned.[12] Unfortunately, some psychiatrists and theologians say that children are born good and society teaches them how to be bad. Scripture teaches that it's the other way around. Children are born with a sinful, human nature and they must be taught to deny their selfish impulses; they must learn to do good. Parents can teach morality using both rewards and punishments. Child psychiatrists call this "behavior modification," using "positive and negative reinforcements." These are just academic terms for what loving parents do when they praise their children for being good and warn them or spank them for being bad. Solomon tells us that "foolishness is bound in the heart of a child; but the rod of correction shall drive it far from him" (Prov. 22:15). Solomon knew about behavior modification three thousand years ago; Moses wrote about it five hundred years before that!

The six-year-old child continues to adopt the conscience of his parents as his own, primarily to gain parental approval, though partially out of fear of punishment. At age twelve or thirteen, he will be more greatly influenced by the morals of his peers rather than parental example. He will choose friends who most closely resemble him in character development. If parents train a child adequately in the first six years of life, they need not fear his choice of friends when he becomes a teenager. Parents

---

12. See Piaget, *The Moral Judgment of the Child.*

like to blame their teenager's behavior on his peers, but this is often an excuse to relieve their own feelings of guilt.

Teenage years

America's teenagers

In May of 1974, a Gallup poll was released, noting that "All signs point to the fact that religion is gaining a new intellectual respectability in this country."[13] Pollster George Gallup, Jr. went on to refer to America's young people, stating that "survey evidence strongly suggests that these groups could well be in the vanguard of religious renewal in this country."

Gallup compared his poll to polls carried out in other nations, and concluded that "the religious character of American youth stands out in bold relief when our young people are compared with the youth of other nations of the world." The United States had the lowest percentage of atheists among its youths—less than 1 percent, compared to 10 percent in France and 12 percent in Sweden. Only 12 percent of American youth say that they have "no interest" in religion, compared to 32 percent in Great Britain, 41 percent in Sweden, and 74 percent in Japan.[14] (It's not surprising that Sweden and Japan are neck-and-neck in a race for the highest suicide rate among teenagers.) Gallup concluded that "American youth are not only exceptionally religious when compared to the youth of other nations but also put a higher premium on 'love and sincerity' as a goal in life and less on 'money and position.' "[15]

13. As reported in the *Durham* (N.C.) *Morning Herald*, May, 1974.
14. Ibid.
15. Ibid.

The search for identity

Teenagers naturally develop strong interests in ideals and ideologies as they search for personal identity. While in this stage of development, they are extremely ripe for spiritual commitments, even though Christianity may have bored them previously. They have a powerful need to strengthen their consciences, and begin to look for reasons and meanings in life.

The spiritual climate of the home

Parents should create a total spiritual atmosphere in the family, with emphasis on positive communication between parents and teenagers. If parents have the right kind of discipline in the home, nagging will be totally unnecessary.

The Jewish people have a religious and family rite that has great potential for emotional and spiritual development. We should consider using a similar ceremony in Christian homes. When a Jewish child reaches his thirteenth birthday, entering the teenage years, Jewish families celebrate what is known as "bar mitzvah" ("son of the commandments") for boys, and "bat (or bas) mitzvah" ("daughter of the commandments") for girls. The family invites all the relatives and close friends to this ceremony, and declares the child a young adult, with increased responsibilities as well as increased freedoms. The parents make a verbal contract with the child, which varies with the creativity of the parents. It has the additional value of reminding the parents that their child is growing up. Parents frequently forget this fact, and continue treating their teenagers as though they were small children. Teenagers can reason like adults, even though they are less mature; our communications with them should show not only our love but also our respect for them as young adults.

A faith of their own

Certain spiritual developments typically take place either in the later teenage years or early twenties. Before the teenage years, children generally accept everything the parents say as truth, and their religious beliefs are largely the religious beliefs of their parents. But during the late teens or early twenties, the individual's greatest need is to feel independent of his parents. Paul Tournier describes this stage in the life of a young person as taking off the "coat" of his parent's morality and "knitting" a coat of his own—at a time when he is basically insecure about his own ability to do so. Tournier states that

> this crisis is necessary and normal. Before he attains adult maturity the young man must go through this time of storm and stress when he has to subject everything to question. The day will come when he will discover again many of the treasures of his childhood, when he will return to the faith in which he grew up and the principles which were inculcated in him. For they were true, and life sees to it that he rediscovers them. But then he will give them a quite personal turn; he will profess them as his own convictions, based upon his innermost experience. In psychology, this is called integration.[16]

This observation helps us to understand Solomon's instruction to "train up a child in the way he should go,

16. Paul Tournier. *The Whole Person in a Broken World*, trans. Helen Doberstein and John Doberstein (New York: Harper & Row, 1964), p. 5.

and when he is old, he will not depart from it" (Prov. 22:6). Solomon doesn't say the individual won't go through a period of doubt in the middle years, but simply that "when he is old, he will not depart from it."

In *The God Who Is There*, Francis Schaeffer emphasizes the need to ground our children in the Word of God and teach them why we believe what we believe. He says we must "communicate Christianity in a way that any given generation can understand.[17] If parents and youth leaders of local churches communicate a living Christianity to their teenagers, along with proofs for the reliability of the Bible, they will greatly ease this normal maturing process for their teenagers.

If teenagers can make it through these rough years, and continue to mature in the Lord, they will have accomplished much. Or rather, they will have allowed God to accomplish much in their lives. They will reap tremendous rewards in feelings of self-worth and self-confidence. The apostle John tells us, "Beloved, if our heart condemn us not, then have we confidence toward God. And whatsoever we ask, we receive of him, because we keep his commandments, and do those things that are pleasing in his sight" (I John 3:21, 22). The greatest gift parents can give their children, from conception to adulthood, is a spiritual base.

17. Francis A. Schaeffer, *The God Who Is There* (Downers Grove, Ill.: InterVarsity, 1968), p. 139.

Two

Genuine Love

What is love? How does it work? Can love be hurt? These are important questions for the family, since love is such a critical part of family foundations.

Agape

In the New Testament, the English word *love* is used to translate two Greek words. The Greek word used in Ephesians 5:25 is *agape*: "Husbands, love your wives, even as Christ also loved the church, and gave himself for it." Dr. Charles R. Smith, a Greek professor, defines *agape* as (1) a concern for the well-being of the one loved, and (2) a volitional choice or determination to act on behalf of the one loved.[1] The *International Standard Bible Encyclopedia* defines *agape* as "an earnest and anxious desire for, and an active and beneficent interest in, the well-being of the

1. Smith, Charles R., "Love is . . . ," *Grace Seminary Spire* (Fall 1976), p. 8.

one loved . . . implying a clear determination of will and judgment."[2] These definitions convey the idea of how *agape* is used in Ephesians 5:25: "Husbands, love your wives [give yourselves to meet their needs], even as Christ also loved [gave himself to meet the real need of] the church." We were sinners who needed to be redeemed; He gave His life, shed His blood, and provided to meet our real need, and that is what love is all about.

Love involves an *act of the will*. The very idea of giving, the very idea of doing something, speaks of action, and whenever we talk about action we are talking about the will being put to work. Love does not begin with feelings; feelings are the fruit of love. There is nothing wrong with romantic feelings—they are indeed beautiful. But love is just like faith in this way. Faith is not feeling, and we counsel people not to depend on their feelings for assurance of their salvation. We are *not* saying it is wrong to have peace, that it is wrong to feel the load lifted. But feelings come and go; they are unpredictable. In the same way, love is not merely a feeling. Feeling is a fruit of love.

In Ephesians 5:25 we have a command. You can't command somebody's feelings. But you can command a person's will. Love—genuine biblical love—can be commanded. In Deuteronomy 6:5 we read: "And thou shalt love the LORD thy God with all thine heart. . . ." That is a command, and it can be obeyed. I John 3:23 states, "And this is his commandment, That we should believe on the name of his Son Jesus Christ, and love one another, as he gave us commandment." The word *commandment* occurs

2. *International Standard Bible Encyclopedia*, vol. III, p. 1932.

several times in this verse. Love can be commanded. Love
is an act of the will. It is the act of giving whatever will
benefit the loved person.

Sometimes a couple may say, "We think our marriage
is over. We want a divorce because we just don't love each
other anymore." But the Bible tells us that a person can
activate his love again. Love may have a way of diminish-
ing, but because it is an act of the will certain things can
be done to build it again. In Revelation 2:4, 5, a local
church that lost its love for the Lord is described: ". . . I
have somewhat against thee, because thou hast left thy
first love." But then the Lord gives them a plan to recover
that love. He says, ". . . do the first works." "DO"—that is
action. They were to do again the things they did when
they first trusted Christ; then they would find their love
flourishing again.

We can apply this approach to the marriage situation.
When one finds his feeling of love in marriage becoming
consistently weak, he or she can take steps to correct it.
Most normal Christians occasionally go through periods
when there is no awareness of the feeling of love for their
mates. This is of no major concern. However, when the
feeling of love is absent for days, weeks, months, or even
years, it becomes a major problem within a marriage.

We must emphasize that lapses in the feeling of love for
a mate are not the result of "fate." Love is not like smog,
floating in and then finally floating out of its own accord.
Love, according to the Bible, is an act of the will. It is the
act of deliberately giving oneself to meeting the needs of
another person. When married partners find their love
weakening, they need to get back to the honeymoon, re-

membering how they acted when they were first married. This may involve the wife dressing up when her husband comes home from work, or cooking a special recipe for him. Or the husband may bring his wife flowers, or take her out on a date, or compliment her.

Bill and Dorothy came to my office for counseling. They stated that they did not feel love for each other anymore. I suggested a project. I had them agree to behave lovingly toward each other for a week. I asked Bill, "If you really felt love toward your wife, what would you do?" He thought of some things and we wrote out a list. Then I asked Dorothy to do the same.

Next, I suggested that for one week they behave as though they felt love for each other, trying to do the things that they had listed. They were not asked to lie to each other, or say "I love you" if they did not feel like it. They were merely asked to choose to behave lovingly toward each other and to act on that choice.

Nearly always when I have suggested this to a couple, they have come back with beaming faces, saying, "the honeymoon is on again." It is just like priming the pump. When some water is put into the pump, it isn't too long before water comes out again in full force. If we want to have love in our homes, we must work at it. It requires responsibly choosing to behave lovingly.

People who say they ought to dissolve their marriage because they don't love each other are showing their ignorance of the Bible. Although this may surprise some people, love is not the primary basis for holding a marriage together. Indeed, this is a misconception based on modern Western social custom, not the Bible. There are no instructions in the Bible on dating, because dating is a modern invention. In Bible times the parents made the arrangements for the son or daughter to marry, and often the day of the wedding was the first time the two ever met. There was no love involved at all, not to mention as the basis for the marriage. The basis was, instead, a contract. It was a contract between the individuals for life, with God as their witness. After they were married, love often did develop.

This is not to say that the present, conventional process of dating, courtship, and marriage is somehow wrong or unbiblical. Of course not. There are many advantages to the present system, and we doubt if even the strictest parents desire to return to the days of arranged marriages. But we must be aware that the popular assumption of romantic love as the sole basis for marriage is an unfortunate one.

When marriage partners find problems developing in their home and in their marriage, they must realize that the true basis of their marriage is not the feeling of love. The basis of their marriage is a covenant, according to Malachi 2:14. They have an agreement; they have a contract with each other, with God as witness, and that narrows down their options. When they "fall out of" love, divorce should not be an option. They should bo concerned to do the will of God, and confine the solutions to their problems within the framework of their covenant. If lack of love is their problem, they can rebuild the marriage by learning how to rebuild the love, instead of throwing it out.

Before you can discover how your love can meet the real needs of your mate, you must understand what the real needs of people are. Below are some of the common, basic needs of human beings.

1. *Acceptance and appreciation.* Everybody needs acceptance and appreciation. We are assured as believers that we are "accepted in the beloved" (Eph. 1:6). Never doubt God's love; never doubt God's acceptance. We are accepted just as Jesus Christ is, because our standing before God is in His righteousness. His acceptance of us is unconditional. But acceptance by and appreciation from one another in marriage is also important. We are loving well when we accept each other without conditions attached to that acceptance.

2. *Purpose in life.* A person needs to know why he is here, where he is needed, and what God has for him to do with his life. God's purpose will never lead a Christian couple apart.

3. *Security and provision.* Both marriage partners need to learn to depend on each other for security and for providing various needs of the family unit.

4. *Loving authority.* Ways to meet this basic need will be amplified in chapter 7.

5. *Individuality.* Each marriage partner should love the mate enough to let him or her develop his or her own likes and dislikes. Since love (agape) "seeketh not her own" (I Cor. 13:5), love will not demand that the mate do everything his or her way.

If one is to obey the Lord by loving his mate, then by acts of the will he must daily give of himself to meet the particular needs of that person the Lord has given him as his married partner.

Phileo

We have looked at one Greek word for love, *agape*. A second word translated "love" in the Bible is *phileo*. In I Peter 1:22, this word is used: "Seeing ye have purified your souls in obeying the truth through the Spirit unto unfeigned *love* of the brethren. . . ." Peter is applying *phileo* to the Christian-to-Christian relationship.

Here is the difference: *Agape* is a one-way street. If the wife does not love the husband, the husband is still commanded by God to love his wife. And he can do so, because *agape* is a unilateral, unconditional love. It takes only one party to exercise this kind of love by giving to meet the needs of the other. God loved us unilaterally before we loved Him. "Herein is love (*agape*), not that we loved (*agape*) God, but that he loved (*agape*) us, and sent his Son to be the propitiation for our sins" (I John 4:10). Love can sometimes be a one-way street, even though unilateral love is not the ideal in a marriage. "God so loved (*agape*) the world, that he gave his only begotten Son . . ."; a person can love regardless of whether or not his marriage partner loves in return. Men are commanded to love their wives and to meet their needs (Eph. 5:25). And wives likewise are instructed to love their husbands (Titus 2:4)

But the word *phileo* is also important when it comes to marriage. This word is *not* unilateral. It is *not* a one-way street; it is reciprocal. One cannot have *phileo* unless both parties are sharing. And the idea of *phileo* is sharing. It is fellowship, communication, commonness of goals, commonness of purpose and of heart. A healthy marriage enjoys the fellowship of *phileo* as well as the dedication of *agape*. But *phileo* takes time together to share feelings, thoughts, and activities. According to a recent survey, the average American couple spends about three minutes a day sharing personally with each other. *Phileo* takes planning and commitment to regular times to share with each other and to continue to date each other, even after the "I do's."

How Love Is Hurt

When people say "I'm hurt," they usually are actually feeling a type of anger; this anger tends to dampen the feeling of love. In I Corinthians 13, the great love chapter of the Bible, Paul gives us some clues concerning the things to avoid if we are to have the proper kind of love.

1. *Love suffereth long.* Obviously, then, a loss of patience will hurt love. Most of us lose our patience from time to time. When we do, it is often because we have developed a set of expectations for others to fulfill. The Bible warns us that when we start making others prisoners of our expectations we are in for disappointment.

   Psalm 62:5 says, "My soul, wait thou only upon God; for my expectation is from him." A good policy for a positive mental attitude is not to *expect* anything from anybody. That way, if we get something from somebody, we will recognize it as a blessing from God, and will praise the Lord for it. But if we expect many things of our mate, he or she will inevitably fall short of our expectations, and we will become angry and impatient. The more perfectionistic we are, the more we will tend to focus on the failures of our mates, rather than the blessings they give us.

I jokingly teach my seminary students "Meier's Rule for Marriage Counseling," that *every couple deserves each other!* When I am impatient with my wife for not living up to my expectations, she reminds me that I deserve her. If we have no expectations except from God, then when others do anything positive, we can praise the Lord. That way, our mental attitude is positive rather than negative.

2. *Love is kind.* Love is characterized by acts of kindness. Conversely, unkindness, sarcasm, or thoughtlessness hurts love.

3. *Love envieth not.* We hurt love when we envy and are jealous of our mates.

4. *Love is not puffed up.* When we lack humility in speech or actions toward our married partner, when we are proud, we are practicing anti-love; we are hurting love. Solomon taught that "only by pride cometh contention" (Prov. 13:10).

5. *Love does not behave itself unseemly.* That simply means that love is not rude. Rudeness, including put-downs, is a form of rejection and will hurt love.

6. *Love seeketh not her own.* It is not self-centered. Self-centeredness demonstrates wrong priorities and will hurt love.

7. *Love is not easily provoked.* An intolerant, chip-on-the-shoulder kind of attitude hurts love.

8. *Love thinketh no evil.* An attitude that likes to review wrongs of the past hurts love. Sometimes when couples argue, they start fishing in the old fish barrel, bringing out things that had long been buried and forgotten. God

forgives and forgets, and so should we. Every day should
be fresh and new.

9. *Love rejoices not in iniquity.* Using other people's evil to
   excuse our own sin hurts love. Saying that everybody is
   doing it so it can't be helped hurts love.

10. *Love beareth all things.* When we begin to attack another
    person's character, calling names, and speaking care-
    lessly, we hurt love. When our mate makes a mistake, we
    must find a polite way of talking and sharing anger, and
    we must be willing to work toward positive measures for
    correction, as well, praying together about the problem.

11. *Love believeth all things, hopeth all things, endureth all
    things.* This word *hope* is very important. An attitude that
    gives up when problems come hurts love. You say "I have
    had it! That is the last straw! That's the end!" That is not
    love. Love hopes. Love is optimistic. Love believes that
    God has a way. Love says, "Lord, help us and we will
    find a solution together."

One of the greatest needs in America today is for strong
Christian homes. Our children need examples of happy
marriages, where the husband and wife work at building
their love, where problems can be solved politely, and
where children are loved and disciplined.

Three

Gut-Level Communication

In marriage counseling, there are two major tasks: (1) helping the married couple resolve their own current conflict; and (2) helping the marriage partners develop better communication skills so they can resolve future conflicts without the help of a pastor or psychiatrist.

It is very difficult to teach communication skills in a book. Like love, communicating takes practice. However, this chapter will attempt to convey some basic communication principles that have helped many of our counselees.

Basic Qualities of Good Communication

As we consider the subject of communication, we want to center our thoughts primarily on several verses from Ephesians that detail the basic qualities of good communication. The first quality of good communication is *truthfulness*. Ephesians 4:25 says, "Wherefore putting away lying, speak every man truth. . . ." There cannot be good communication unless there is this desire on both parties

39

to be truthful. In Ephesians 4:15, Christians are told, "But speaking the truth in love, [we] may grow up into him in all things, which is the head, even Christ." There is no better advice anywhere for mate-to-mate, parent-to-parent, friend-to-friend, or any other type of communication than, "Speak the truth in love." If more Christians practiced this, we would see believers grow in Christ-likeness. Speaking the truth, sharing with openness and freedom what is on one's heart, is one of the qualities essential for good communication.

The second quality is *handling anger properly*. Ephesians 4:26 says, "Be ye angry, and sin not." There are two ways of handling anger incorrectly. We do wrong and we sin when we handle anger by losing our temper ("blowing up"). That is suggested by the last word in verse 26, *wrath*. "Blowing up" immediately cuts the communication lines. There is another wrong way of handling anger and that is by quietly pouting ("clamming up"). That is also suggested in verse 26 when it says, "let not the sun go down upon your wrath." When there is irritation and anger inside, the problem should be talked out. Communicate! Don't let it smolder. Don't suppress it. Don't put off discussing it. Deal with it, and deal with it by sundown. The handling of anger biblically is so vital for physical, mental, emotional, and spiritual health that we include an entire section later in this chapter called "Dealing with Anger Biblically" (pp. 46–60).

The third basic quality of good communication is *maintaining proper attitudes*. There are some wrong attitudes that will certainly cut off communication, not just in marriage but in all one's personal relationships. Some wrong attitudes are listed in Ephesians 4:29; the first word that suggests such an attitude is the word *corrupt*.

The word *corrupt* means "rotten."[1] It is an attitude that shows a person just doesn't care. "Let no corrupt communication proceed out of your mouth. . . ." There are other wrong attitudes listed in verse 31. *Bitterness* means "pricking, hatred, displaying hatred, sharpness."[2] The word *wrath* indicates another attitude problem. That means "passion,"[3] or losing one's temper. The word *anger* means "displeasure,"[4] and *clamor* means "the tumult or controversy."[5] It comes from a Greek word which means the "cry of a raven."

Another bad attitude is described by the phrase *evil speaking*. These words mean defamatory speech; one is speaking evil when he puts people down. The Bible is clear that we should "speak not evil one of another," (James 4:11). That means we should not defame people, hurt their reputation, talk about their faults to anyone except to them personally (and even then we must do so without the poor attitudes that we are discussing here). *Malice* is another negative attitude found in the last part of verse 31. A malicious person is one who is "vicious in character."[6]

This passage in Ephesians 4 also describes some right attitudes we should have in communication. In the last

1. W. E. Vine, *An Expository Dictionary of New Testament Words* (Old Tappan, N.J.: Revell, 1966), p. 243.
2. Ibid., p. 129.
3. Ibid., p. 239.
4. Ibid., p. 55.
5. Ibid., p. 194.
6. Ibid., p. 32.

part of verse 29 we find the word *edifying*. Edifying means "building."[7] When we apply this to our spiritual lives it means "life-building." When we edify we help stimulate another to grow in grace; we build up the other's life. We see how this is to be done in the rest of verse 29. We are to use our mouth to edify, and use our communication to build up, "that it may minister grace unto the hearers." One measure for determining if we are edifying is whether or not our speech ministers grace. Grace in the believer's life involves the desire and the power to do God's will (Phil 2:13). Paul said, "but I laboured more abundantly than they all: yet not I, but the grace of God which was with me" (I Cor. 15:10). Does our communication with our married partner or with another Christian help build up their desire and give them the power to do God's will? Or, by our communication do we drag them down and decrease their power and desire to do God's will? Job's wife, for example, told Job to curse God and die (Job 2:9), which I'm sure was not very encouraging!

Another right attitude is *kindness*. We are to be kind one to another, as Paul says in Ephesians 4:32. Quality communication includes the attitude of kindness. This word means to treat others with an attitude that is "pleasant, good, and gracious."[8] Husband and wife ought to speak with a pleasant, gracious attitude toward each other. "Love covereth all sins" (Prov. 10:12). A loving, kind spirit ought to be there.

7. Ibid., p. 18.
8. Ibid., p. 185.

Another positive attitude mentioned in verse 32 is *tender-heartedness*. The word *tenderhearted* means "compassionate."[9] We are also instructed here to forgive one another. How much should we forgive? "As God for Christ's sake hath forgiven you." That is total forgiveness.

Basic Procedures for Communication

Under normal conditions and in most situations, the first procedure for good communication is to *take time*. There cannot be good communication without making time for it. This idea goes back to our previous examination of what love really is according to the Scriptures. Love is *agape* and love is *phileo*. *Agape* means that actions are constructed to benefit the needs of the other person. But *phileo* requires the involvement of at least two people in order to really function. It means sharing and fellowshiping together. But if *agape* and *phileo* are to be practiced in the marriage relationship, one must make time for sharing and talking.

The husband and wife should set aside time together each day. One good time would be during devotions. Another time would be after the children are in bed, when parents are more free to sit, hold hands, and talk about whatever is on their hearts—opening up and sharing what God has done for them that day. Praying is a beautiful way of opening communication lines.

9. Ibid.

Often couples who have had severe problems with communication have tried "sentence praying" together. The partners hold hands across from each other, while one begins to pray—only one sentence. Then the other prays a one-sentence prayer. They continue to take turns until they have both shared everything that is on their hearts with God and consequently with their partner. Many couples we have counseled have said that sentence praying has transformed their communication problems. If a couple can communicate together with God, they can communicate with each other—but they need to make time for it. A date once a week with one's mate is a beautiful time not just to have fun (although that's part of it), but also to communicate in a relaxed setting, away from the normal pressures.

You may ask, "What about conflicts that come up when we're talking?" Couples sometimes face problems and don't resolve them or don't know how to resolve them. The goal of good communication is to have both the husband and wife face the problem and focus on it together, rather than attacking each other or arguing about "who's right." Thus the basic procedures for communication are (1) take time to communicate, and (2) focus on the problem rather than attacking each other. A third basic procedure is to be willing to take the initiative. Don't wait for your partner to take the first step. Matthew 5:23, 24 instructs, "Therefore if thou bring thy gift to the altar, and there rememberest that thy brother hath ought against thee; [You] leave there thy gift before the altar, and go thy way; first be reconciled to thy brother, and then come and offer thy gift."

What if someone else has offended you? The Bible says you still are to take the initiative. It is still your burden, your responsibility. Matthew 18:15 says, "Moreover if thy brother shall trespass against thee, [you] go and tell him his fault between thee and him alone: if he shall hear thee, thou hast gained thy brother." Here you haven't done the offending; it is the other party who has done something wrong. It would be natural to assume that the other person should come and ask you for forgiveness. But don't wait; you initiate the communicating. You go to him or her and take the initiative. Open yourself up; be vulnerable.

You can't restore communication unless you approach your partner in a spirit of meekness; you must be a spiritual person yourself. If you are a godly person, it is your burden and your responsibility to take the initiative when you have offended the other party in the marriage (Matt. 5:23). And if someone else has offended you to the point that it is robbing you of your peace, then you again are to take the initiative (Matt. 18:15).

If most of the problems in a marriage are communication problems, then it certainly should not be too difficult to get the marriage partners on a corrective path toward resolving those problems. However, it must be added that therapy to work on communicating in love on a gut level can require fifty or more one-hour counseling sessions for couples who never communicated well with their families when they were growing up. We would encourage couples like this to be patient. The expense and effort will certainly be worth it in the long run.

There are so many blessings that come from proper communication that it would be hard to list them all. Communication in the marriage, in the Christian home, results in a *clear conscience*. That is one of the basic needs of every human being. One cannot genuinely love as he should, as God wants him to, unless he practices clearing the air and clearing the conscience. This is done by communication.

Another blessing is *a flow of information* in the home. People who have access to all the facts can make intelligent decisions. God put husband and wife together to complement one another, to match one another, and to build a great team together.

By communication we develop our own *spiritual life*. Every one of us is commanded by the Lord to grow in grace and to develop a Christ-like maturity. One cannot adequately and properly mature without learning to think, communicate, and share his feelings. When one is able to share and relate, he finds himself growing and maturing in Christ-likeness. Solomon told us over three thousand years ago that, "[as] iron sharpeneth iron; so a man sharpeneth the countenance of his friend" (Prov. 27:17). God uses mates and true friends who are willing to "speak the truth in love"—to confront us truthfully yet tactfully about our blind spots—in order to "sharpen us" toward Christ-likeness.

Dealing with Anger Biblically

In *Happiness Is a Choice*, by Paul Meier and Frank Minirth (Baker, 1978), the authors outline seven basic guidelines for a happy life (chapter 12). The third of those seven guidelines was discussed as a very crucial one, "getting rid of grudges." The communication section of this book is a good place to review some of the principles involved in dealing with anger biblically.

Appropriate or Inappropriate Anger

Whenever you feel any significant anger toward yourself, God, or anybody else, you will best handle that anger if you immediately analyze whether it is appropriate or inappropriate. That way, you will gain insight into your anger. Some anger is an appropriate response (righteous indignation) when someone has sinned against us. Examples would include a "friend" spreading gossip or lies about us. Or a mate refusing to have sex. According to I Corinthians 7:3-5, a Christian husband and wife should never turn each other down for sex except when they have agreed for a time to fast and pray. They each have a right to the other's body. If a wife refuses her husband (and the reverse holds true as well), she is violating his God-given right, and it would be appropriate for him to have some righteous indignation (appropriate anger). He must, however, forgive her by bedtime (whether she "deserves" forgiveness or not).

In Ephesians 4:26, we are commanded to "be angry, and sin not" (the Greek verb is in the imperative mood—a command). The same verse, however, warns us that we should never let the sun go down on our wrath. We must not hold grudges. We must be rid of the dangerous emotion of anger by sundown, or bedtime. Obviously, if all anger were sinful, we would not be commanded by God's Word to "be angry and sin not."

But much of our anger is sinful and inappropriate. There are three main sources of sinful (inappropriate) anger:

1. Anger that results when one's selfish demands are not met. Selfishness is the root of most inappropriate anger. The more selfish a person is (whether he is openly or subtly selfish), the angrier he will be much of the time. He will have serious problems with depression because holding grudges is a main cause of depression.

2. Anger that results when one's perfectionistic demands are not being satisfied. Perfectionists (obsessive-compulsives) expect too much from themselves, from others, and even from God. As a result, they are frequently angry with themselves, others, or God—but mostly with themselves. That's why perfectionist personality types have the highest rate of depression.

3. Anger that results from suspiciousness. When a person has a few paranoid personality traits, he will frequently misinterpret the motives of others. Someone will not notice him, and he will assume that person was purposely avoiding him. Someone will tease him slightly in an attempt to win his friendship, but he will assume that person was actually cutting him down. An individual with paranoid tendencies is so blind to his own repressed anger that he projects it, and mistakenly thinks that others are feeling angry toward him. The Bible discusses projection in several places, but especially in Matthew 7:3-5, where Christ Himself states:

> And why do you look at the speck in your brother's eye, but do not notice the log that is in your own eye? Or how can you say to your brother, "Let me take the speck out of your eye," and behold, the log is in your own eye? You hypocrite, first take the log out of your own eye, and then

you will see clearly enough to take the speck out of your brother's eye. (NASB).

As we can see from Christ's illustration, sometimes our brother really does have a speck in his eye. But even then we may blow it out of proportion because of the log in our own. In other words, we may get extremely angry over a minor matter because there is a superabundance of repressed anger in ourselves. Or, perhaps our brother's sin reminds us of a sin we are guilty of but are lying to ourselves about. Psychiatrists have long recognized that the kind of person we become most angry at is probably our own personality type. We humans lie to ourselves so much about our own faults (our blind spots) that when we meet someone with similar faults, we find ourselves reacting negatively to him, though we do not understand why. All people do this, but paranoid personalities are especially so disposed.

Anger toward God is always inappropriate, since God claims in Psalm 103 to be perfectly fair, righteous, and loving in all that He does. Whenever we feel angry toward God, we should talk to Him about it, realizing that our anger toward God is purely the result of our own human naiveté or selfishness. We must trust God completely to do what is best for us in the long run, instead of being naively angry at Him for not answering a certain prayer our way.

It should be obvious by now that insights into the appropriateness or inappropriateness of our anger can be extremely valuable. If we could, through Christian maturity, eliminate most of our inappropriate anger by giving up our selfishness, perfectionistic demands, and suspicion, we would eliminate a majority of our anger.

Such insight can be a tremendous help in overcoming depression. Of course, it is first necessary for an individual to recognize the fact that he is angry. Anger is hard to deal with unless an individual realizes it is there. Once he recognizes his anger, understanding why he becomes angry in certain situations helps him to control and handle his anger better in the future. For example, perhaps he becomes extremely angry when a friend seems to slight him. If his anger is out of proportion to the actual event, it may be because the event reminded him of another period in his life when he felt inferior and inadequate. The current event reinforced those past feelings and insecurities. Perhaps 25 percent of his response is to the current situation, and the other 75 percent is his reaction to feelings that were long ago repressed.

Insight into a person's past and how it affected him can be of tremendous help in overcoming anger and depression in the present. Insight into one's current personality traits can also be of help in overcoming anger and depression. One word of caution, however—insight can be dangerous. If insight is given when a person is not prepared to handle it, or if it is given too quickly, it can be extremely painful. Some people who gain too much insight too rapidly become psychotic in order to cope with the reality they have learned. In their psychotic state, they live in unreality, and all their insights are blocked out. Thus, insight must be given and used with caution, especially in the cases of unstable individuals. Remember to "speak the truth in love."

Verbalizing Anger

If you are convinced that your anger is appropriate, you will verbalize that anger and forgive the object of that anger by bedtime. This is in obedience to Matthew 5:21-24 and Ephesians 4:26. In Christ's Sermon on the Mount, He gives us the following instructions:

> You have heard that the ancients were told, "You shall not commit murder" and "Whoever commits murder shall be liable to the court." But I say to you that every one who is angry with his brother shall be guilty before the court; and whoever shall say to his brother, "Raca [good for nothing]," shall be guilty before the supreme court; and whoever shall say, "You fool," shall be guilty enough to go into the hell of fire. If therefore you are presenting your offering at the altar, and there remember that your brother has something against you, leave your offering there before the altar, and go your way; first be reconciled to your brother, and then come and present your offering (Matt. 5:21-24, NASB).

What a fantastic illustration Christ uses here. We humans measure our "super-spirituality" by publicly putting a large offering in a collection plate. But Christ tells us to demonstrate our genuine spirituality by loving our brother enough to face him, no matter how painful that may be, and resolve any anger we have toward him. If our brother is angry toward us, Christ still makes it our responsibility to go to him and reconcile with him. That takes great courage, and an abundance of Christian maturity and love.

Why does Christ want us to verbalize our anger? There are several psychological and spiritual benefits that result:

1. It helps us to be aware of the truth—that we really are feeling angry—instead of repressing it and wondering why we feel so frustrated or depressed.

2. It helps us forgive. It is possible to forgive someone without verbalizing our anger, but verbalizing makes forgiving a great deal easier, even if the person does not agree that our anger is appropriate. We must forgive no matter what response we get from the other person. Why should we suffer depression for his sin? That would be foolish. We should verbalize our anger and forgive him whether he deserves forgiveness or not. This is an act of obedience to God's Word and will keep us from becoming depressed. God doesn't want us to hold grudges because He wants us to experience love, joy, and peace.

3. God will use our verbalization, if done tactfully (speaking the truth in love), to convict our brother of sin in his life. Anger should always be verbalized tactfully. The intent of verbalizing anger should always be to reconcile our brother, never to get vengeance.

4. Tactfully verbalizing our anger produces intimacy in a marriage or in a friendship. If we don't verbalize our anger, we will almost certainly end up showing our anger nonverbally through passive (and usually unconscious) games—pouting, procrastinating, burning supper, developing a headache when it's time for sex, coming home late and "forgetting" to call, and so on.

5. The person to whom we tactfully verbalize our anger will nearly always respect us much more for being assertive, in control of our emotions, and responsible in handling our anger.

6. It helps prevent gossip. If we don't verbalize our anger to the person toward whom we feel anger, the temptation to tell others about how that person has offended us will be almost overwhelming. If we do verbalize our anger, this will also help keep the other person from gossiping about us. Instead, we will resolve the conflict—or at least bring it out in the open. It is better to be wounded by a knife than to be hurt by someone's tongue. Several of the seven sins God hates the most (Prov. 6) involve pride, gossiping, and sowing discord among the brethren. God hates gossip; He loves resolution of conflicts.

Let us note that God does not legalistically require each Christian to verbalize every tidbit of anger he feels to every single person toward whom he feels it. A believer must use his judgment and be practical. For example, you do not storm into the Oval Office to confront the President of the United States if you disagree with some decision he has made. If verbalizing your anger toward your boss would mean losing your job, you may choose to verbalize to God the anger you feel toward your boss; ask God to help you forgive your boss whether he deserves forgiveness or not.

At other times, it might be very appropriate to tactfully share your anger with your boss, or even to send a telegram of protest to the President of the United States concerning one of his decisions. Again, use your judgment and pray for discretion. When angry at your boss, you may find that sharing the problem with your mate later that day will help you bring the problem into focus and enable you to choose to forgive him. Some physical activity such as jogging or tennis can also help you to ventilate enough

of the anger to bring it into perspective, and you can forgive. But though athletics can be a good assistant, be sure
never to use athletics exclusively to deal with your anger.
Even watching contact sports like football can help you
symbolically ventilate part of your anger. But that is not
enough. You will certainly get depressed if you hold
enough grudges for a long enough time.

Ideally, anger should be ventilated both to God (on a
vertical level) and men (on a horizontal level). God is the
only one who has supernatural power to deal with our
anger. A psychiatrist doesn't, even though he has an M.D.—
that magical degree that some patients think stands for
"Master Deity." If you are depressed, pray every night that
God will reveal to you any unconscious grudges you may
be holding against someone—including yourself. Only God
can do that.

This discussion on verbalizing anger would not be complete without considering the two extremes used to express anger. When we are overly aggressive with our anger,
we rid ourselves of our own feelings and vent our anger
at someone else's expense. We attack his character; we
attack him personally. The other extreme when expressing
anger is to be passive. We do not directly express the way
we feel, but we take out our anger in some kind of "ma-
neuver," such as putting things off, pouting, doing a poor
job, letting others run our lives and at the same time re-
senting it, and saying yes when we really want to say no.
Neither extreme is healthy.

The healthy balance is found in assertiveness. When we
are assertive, we do express the way we feel, but we use
love and tact in what we say. We say yes when we mean

yes and we say no when we mean no. We stand up for what we think we should stand up for, and we ask for what we feel is important. An example may prove helpful. If someone hurt our feelings and we were aggressive, we would attack him personally and attack his character by saying insulting things to him. If we were passive, we would not say anything but simply pout about it (and perhaps talk to other people about him behind his back). If we were assertive we would go to him and say something to this effect: "I've been feeling angry about what you said, but I would like for us to resolve our differences. Can we talk about it?"

Remember that no matter how you verbalize your anger, you must forgive! Forgiving starts with an act of the will. Forgiving is a choice. It may take some time to work through the emotional feelings that are involved, for we cannot merely dismiss our feelings. It takes time to reprogram our "computer" of feelings. However, we can forgive others immediately by an act of the will. This distinction between an act of the will and the emotional feelings involved is an important one. It is also important to remember that forgiving does not mean to erase all memory of the offense. Rather, it means not to charge the offense to someone's account. God the Father forgives us of all our sins because of what Christ did on the cross for us. This means that He no longer holds our sins against us. He no longer charges them to our account. Logic tells us that if forgiveness meant erasing all recall, we would all be in trouble. However, forgiveness means no longer holding something against someone else's account.

There are basically six groups of people which are often the objects of our anger and which we need to forgive. First, there is often much repressed anger toward our parents. We need to remember that God can cause difficult situations of the past to work together for good. We need to remember that we, too, will make mistakes in raising our children. We need to forgive our parents for mistakes and sins they committed when they were raising us, whether they deserve our forgiveness or not.

Second, we need to forgive ourselves. Just as we get angry with other people, we become angry with ourselves for making mistakes and for not doing better. We are often critical of ourselves and are harder on ourselves than we are on other people. We need to forgive ourselves for past mistakes and sins. God is aware of our weaknesses. He knows we are but dust (Ps. 103:14). He says that when He removes our sins, they are as far from us as the east is from the west (verse 12). He wants us to do the same and no longer hold our past mistakes against ourselves.

Third, we need to deal with our repressed anger toward God. We do not forgive God, for God has done nothing wrong; but we may have repressed anger or bitter feelings toward Him. We may subconsciously reason somewhat as follows: "After all, He is God, and He could have prevented or corrected the situation if He had chosen to." Like Job we need to confess our anger toward God, talk with Him about it, and ask Him to help us resolve it.

Fourth, we need to deal with repressed anger toward our mate. We need to forgive him or her for mistakes he or she has made. When two individuals live together, many anger-arousing situations occur, and anger can build up over a period of time. An individual needs to forgive in order to prevent depression.

Fifth, we need to forgive those in authority over us. Anger often builds toward authority figures in our lives. We need to forgive them for whatever wrong we feel they may have done us. God has put them in authority over us. We need to respond to them and learn to talk with them about how we feel. Under no circumstances should we hold grudges against them.

The sixth category of those whom we need to forgive is simply classified as "others." There are often many other people in our lives whom we need to forgive. This group may include our peers when we were young. Various situations may have occurred long ago, and the repressed feelings and anger were never dealt with. The anger needs to be confessed and the person(s) forgiven.

God has said much about anger and the need to control it. One of the best ways to control anger is to continue to grow in Christ. As we grow in Christ and in humility, much of the anger will automatically dissipate, and we will be happier, healthier individuals.

If, after analyzing your anger, you discover that your anger is inappropriate—the result of your selfishness, perfectionism, or suspiciousness—then verbalization of your inappropriate anger will probably not be necessary. However, sometimes it is helpful to verbalize your inappropriate anger. For example:

Friend, a little while ago I was feeling angry with you, so I prayed about it and analyzed it. After thinking about it for the past couple of hours, I decided I was letting my perfectionism get out of hand. I was expecting you to be perfect, and started to get upset when you didn't do everything perfectly. Will you forgive me for being so petty? You'll probably have to put up with some pettiness in me if you really want to be my good friend.

As has been discussed earlier, the best way to get rid of inappropriate anger is to give up the source of inappropriate anger—selfishness, perfectionism, and suspiciousness.

The Vengeance Motive

Leave all vengeance to God. Never "get even" with anyone, including yourself.

There is only one motive for retaining anger (holding grudges), and that single motive is vengeance. Recently a patient came to our office to gain some insight into his past three years of depression. He was asked if there was anyone he had been especially angry with three years ago, that is, just prior to the beginning of his depression. Though initially surprised at the question, after thinking about it for less than a minute, he appeared to be getting angry. His neck became blotchy and red, his pupils began to dilate, and his fingers began to draw into a fist. He began swearing as he described a teacher who, three years ago, in front of his college peers, had accused him of cheating, though he was innocent. He described the incident with vivid hostility. When asked, "Why don't you forgive your teacher? It will help you get over your depression," he replied angrily, "Absolutely not! I'll never forgive her till the day I die. She doesn't deserve it!"

At that point it seemed appropriate to gently poke fun at the patient, to help him see the absurdity of his position: "You're really punishing her, aren't you! You're going through three years of depression to get your vengeance. Is it worth it? Do you think she even remembers who you are?" The mechanisms of depression were explained to him—how biochemical changes are brought on by holding grudes. Here was also a marvelous opportunity to share Christ with him. After developing a relationship with Christ, and using Christ's power to help him forgive his teacher (though she didn't "deserve" forgiveness), he got over his depression in a matter of weeks after suffering from its symptoms for three years.

Vengeance is a poor motive. If one has any faith in God, personal vengeance is totally unnecessary and foolish. God will wreak vengeance on all who deserve it—or else He will show His divine grace and forgive them, especially if they have repented. But whether God shows vengeance or divine grace, that is God's decision. It's none of your concern. Stay out of God's business! We humans spend half our lives trying to be God in various ways.

Let's look at what the apostle Paul said about vengeance in Romans 12:17-21:

Never pay back evil for evil to anyone. Respect what is right in the sight of all men. If possible, so far as it depends on you, be at peace with all men. Never take your own revenge, beloved, but leave room for the wrath of God, for it is written, *"Vengeance is Mine, I will repay, says the LORD. But if your enemy is hungry, feed him, and if he is thirsty, give him a drink; for in so doing you will heap burning coals* upon his head." Do not be overcome by evil, but overcome evil with good (NASB).

God's Word is so beautiful, and His ways are so wise. If we proud humans would only forgive others when they wrong us, and forgive ourselves when we make mistakes, we would never suffer the pains of depression.

Thus we have discussed three major principles for dealing with anger: (1) Gain insight into whether your anger is appropriate or inappropriate; (2) verbalize your significant, appropriate anger, and forgive before bedtime; (3) never try to get vengeance on anyone—leave that to God.

Guidelines for "Fighting Fair" in Marriage

The best advice to give any idealistic young couple about to get married is to remind them that no one is perfect. All humans are selfish at times. All humans exhibit false pride at times. *Every Christian married couple has conflicts and disagreements.* If a married couple claims they haven't had any disagreements in years, *one of them isn't necessary.* One of them has put his (or her) brain on a shelf and has let the other think for both.

Many mature, godly adults have admitted to us privately that it took five or more years of frequent marital conflicts before they arrived at a satisfactory marriage with satisfactory communication habits. We wrote this chapter because we hate to see our Christian brothers and sisters suffering such needless emotional pain. We hate to see the effects of marital conflicts on innocent children. Following are some proven guidelines for "fighting fair" in a healthy Christian marriage:[10]

1. Sincerely commit your lives to Jesus Christ as Lord.
2. Consider the marriage a life-long commitment, just as Christ is eternally committed to His bride, the church.
3. Agree to always listen to each other's feelings, even if you disagree with the appropriateness of those feelings.
4. Commit yourselves to both honesty and acceptance.
5. Determine to attempt to love each other *unconditionally*, with each partner assuming 100 percent of the responsibility for resolving marital conflicts (the 50/50 concept seldom works).
6. Consider all the factors in a conflict before bringing it up with your mate.
7. Confess any personal sin in the conflict to Christ before confronting your mate.
8. Limit the conflict to the here and now—*never bring up past failures*, since all past failures should already have been forgiven.
9. Eliminate the following phrases from your vocabulary:
   a. "You never" or "You always"
   b. "I can't" (always substitute "I won't")
   c. "I'll try" (usually means "I'll make a half-hearted effort but won't quite succeed").
   d. "You should" or "You shouldn't" (these are parent-to-child statements)
10. Limit the discussion to the one issue that is the center of the conflict.
11. Focus on that issue rather than attacking each other.

10. Most of these guidelines are based on "Successful Conflict Resolution in the Christian Life," unpublished counseling handout by Frank B. Wichern, Ph.D., Dallas Theological Seminary.

12. Ask your mate if he would like some time to think about the conflict before discussing it (but never put it off past bedtime—see Eph. 4:26).

13. Each mate should use "I feel . . ." messages, expressing his response to whatever words or behavior aroused the conflict. For example, "*I feel* angry toward you for coming home late for supper without calling me first" is an adult-to-adult message, whereas "*You should* always call me when you're going to be late for supper" is a parent-to-child message. A parent-to-child message will cause the mate to become defensive.

14. Never say anything derogatory about your mate's personality. Proverbs 11:12 tells us that "he who despises [belittles] his neighbor lacks sense" (NASB).

15. Even though your mate won't always be correct, consider your mate an instrument of God, working in your life. Proverbs 12:1 says, "He who hates reproof is stupid" (NASB).

16. Never counterattack, even if your mate does not follow these guidelines.

17. Don't tell your mate why you think he or she does what he does (unless he asks you), but rather stick to how you feel about what he does.

18. Don't try to read your mate's mind. If you're not sure what he meant by something he said, ask him to clarify it.

19. Commit yourselves to follow the instructions carefully in the "Dealing with Anger Biblically" section of this chapter. This will help you avoid depression, which results in increased irritability and increased marital conflicts.

20. Be honest about your true emotions, but keep them under control. Proverbs 29:11 says, "A fool always loses his temper, but a wise man holds it back" (NASB). Proverbs 15:18 says, "A hot-tempered man stirs up strife, but the slow to anger pacifies contention (NASB).

21. Remember that the resolution of the conflict is what is

important, *not* who wins or loses. If the conflict is re-
solved, you both win. You're on the same team, not op-
posing, competing teams.

22. Agree with each other on what topics are "out of bounds"
because they are too hurtful or have already been discussed (for example, in-laws, continued obesity, and so
on).

23. Pray about each conflict before discussing it with your
mate.

24. Commit yourselves to carefully learn and practice these
24 guidelines for "fighting fair" in marriage and agree
with each other to call "foul" whenever one of you ac-
cidentally or purposefully breaks one of these guidelines.
(You may even choose to agree on a dollar fine for each
violation!)

Four

Discipline

Another aspect of a happy, successful, Christian home is children. Ephesians 6:1-4 is the familiar passage which deals with children:

> Children, obey your parents in the Lord: for this is right. Honour thy father and mother; which is the first commandment with promise; that it may be well with thee, and thou mayest live long on the earth. And, ye fathers, provoke not your children to wrath: but bring them up in the nurture and admonition of the Lord.

Factors for Success

Most people agree that we need to love our children and that we need to discipline our children. But that isn't enough. That still won't produce good children; that still won't produce good leadership. Many parents have really missed the mark where the child's sense of self-worth or self esteem is concerned. The guidelines in this chapter show how to build healthy self-concepts in your children. For more information on this subject, we would refer you to Paul Meier's *Christian Child-Rearing and Personality Development* (Baker, 1977). The writings of Bruce Narramore, Maurice Wagner and James Dobson are also extremely helpful in the area of understanding the roots of self-concept problems and how to overcome them.

Let us examine the Ephesians 6 passage further. In verse 4, the word nurture means "discipline."[1] So love needs to be coupled with discipline. Discipline, however, does not simply mean spanking. It can also mean "a structured training." It implies training through experience. This includes spanking, but does not end there.

Admonition means "the training by word."[2] It implies not merely setting the rules and the penalties or the rewards, but instructing. One of the father's responsibilities is to sit down and explain, to teach, to encourage and tell why and wherefore, and to use the Scriptures, and to build the children from within.

The word *provoke* means "to arouse to anger."[3] Fathers are not to exasperate their children by having unrealistic expectations of them or by inconsistent discipline.

Children who constantly feel unable to please their parents will not develop a healthy self-concept (self-esteem). They have their minds and hearts filled with negative feelings. They have a lot of trouble getting their faith going.

---

1. W. E. Vine, *An Expository Dictionary of New Testament Words*, (Old Tappan, N.J.: Revell, 1966), p. 183.
2. Ibid., p. 30.
3. Ibid., p. 228.

They say, "I can't do this, I can't do that, I can't do anything right. Everything I try to do fails." When they give up, it is because they are plagued with an inferiority complex, and that comes from their home. It comes from a lack of proper instruction. It comes from a lack of proper relationship with the father, as well as other factors.

We can see how this is true from the following case study:[4] A certain young boy's mother was a large woman, a dominating person who displayed no love for anyone. She had been married three times (her second husband divorced her because she abused him). The little fellow never experienced any love or discipline. He was just shoved around. In fact, the mother told him, "Don't ever bother me at work. I don't want you bothering me." He was totally rejected. He did have a high I.Q., but when he was old enough he dropped out of high school. Then he saw a sign that said "The Marines can make a man out of you."

"That's what I need," he said, and joined the Marines. But he failed there when he was given a dishonorable discharge. He had no talent, no skill—he didn't even have a driver's license.

Later he had a chance to visit a foreign country. While he was there he met and married a lady who was an illegitimate child. After a while, their marriage began to fail. His wife started to push him around, and finally she told him to get out of the house. He felt so rejected by his

4. James Dobson, *Hide or Seek*, (Old Tappan, N.J.: Revell, 1971), pp. 9-11.

wife that he got down on his hands and knees and begged her to let him come back into the house. They returned to the United States.

The only talent he had was shooting a rifle. On November 22, 1963, he used his talent in the third story of a book storage building in Dallas, Texas. His name was Lee Harvey Oswald. Now look at his life: his home life neglected to give him three important factors: love, discipline, and a sense of self-worth.

Following are some basic ways of implementing these three essentials. A survey was conducted some years ago by a psychology professor. He wrote to some Christian leaders who had been successful in rearing their own children. Here is what various successful parents recommended:

Love

1. *Spend time with your children.* There ought to be a time every week when the entire family gets together just for fun, recreation, fellowship, and sharing love. There should be a strong relationship between the father and both male and female children. Each child will benefit from a "date" with the father at least once a month. The father should regularly take each child out alone to eat or participate in some type of recreational activity, just to show his love and to talk. This builds tremendous self-worth in the child.
2. *Try to win them to Christ when they are young.* If your children know you are concerned, that you want them to go to heaven, that you want them to have their sins forgiven and have Jesus as their personal Savior, they will know you love them.
3. *Frequently hug them and tell them you love them.* You've seen the bumper sticker that says, "Have you hugged your

kids today?" That needs to be asked every day. I hugged a grown man recently and he broke down sobbing. His wife said, "He has never been hugged by a man before in his life—not even his father." Many children and young people would probably have to say the same thing: "I can't remember my dad ever putting his arm on my shoulder. I can't remember my dad ever saying to me, 'I like you' or 'I love you.' " If you have children in your home, make sure you let them know you love them. If they are too self-conscious to let you hug them, grab them once in awhile and hug them anyway. They'll get used to it!

Discipline (Training)

1. *Teach them to memorize Scriptures.* Get your children to memorize verses that will build character in their lives.
2. *Set standards and guidelines about the company they keep.* Guidelines are part of discipline. This is especially important for the teen years.
3. *Prepare them ahead of time to counteract the pressures of public opinion.* Young people can fall when they suddenly face a world they have not been prepared for. They need to be able to counteract the pressures of the world. They need to be prepared for what they will do when their friends offer them a cigarette, marijuana and other drugs, or when they are alone with a date in a parked car. They need to discuss these pressures with parents before they are facing them personally. They need to know why they believe what they believe.
4. *Consistently discipline them when they need it.* Consistency is the key word here. Consistency means that the husband and wife agree on matters of discipline (we will discuss this in more detail in chapter 5).

Self-worth

1. *Have brief, interesting family devotions.* Sharing should be encouraged, and every member of the family, including

the children, should take a part. Let the children pray, too. Let them share a testimony, a sad feeling, or a blessing. The idea of sharing is extremely important to a sense of self-worth.

2. *Develop their cultural and athletic talents.* If children are good at sports, help them and encourage them. Be there as often as you can when they play. Teach them to play the piano or some other musical instrument if they are musically inclined.

3. *Compliment character qualities and honest effort.* There is nothing wrong with parents saying, "My, you look nice today," complimenting appearance. But make sure your *emphasis* is on the inward qualities, "I saw the way you treated Suzie. You gave her your doll. What a generous person you are." Tell your children how you see them and they will be what you see. Compliment their character. This builds self-worth.

Discipline of Younger Children

There are some definite benefits the Lord promises us as the result of administration of physical discipline. Some people do not believe in physical discipline; they think it is outdated. But the Bible makes it clear that there are benefits one needs to be aware of.

Physical discipline *imparts wisdom.* Most people want their children to be wise. Proverbs 29:15 says, "The rod and reproof give wisdom. . . ." If people believed the Bible, and wanted their children to be wise, they would spank them when they did wrong. The last part of verse 15 notes another fringe benefit, and that is the promise of a *happy future.* A negative warning is given in verse 15, but its reverse can readily be inferred to see the benefit: ". . . a child left to himself bringeth his mother to shame." Many people have the wrong philosophy: let children do their own thing; don't scold them; don't stop them; don't make them disappointed or sad. No! If a child is wrong, the loving parent will correct him. If he defies parental authority, a loving parent will spank him. If he is left to himself, he will bring shame to the parents. But if a child is well-disciplined, he will in all probability have a happy future.

Proverbs 23:14 states another benefit of physical discipline is that it will *help to save his soul*. "Thou shalt beat him with the rod, and shalt deliver his soul from hell." If parents teach their child that there are consequences connected with rebellion, it will be easier for him to respond to the gospel; he has already practiced surrendering to his parents. But if his parents leave him to himself and don't correct him, he may be just as hard and rebellious toward God when he hears the gospel as he was toward his parents. They can help him to trust Christ if they prepare him for the message of salvation by being godly parents.

Administering the Discipline

The wrong way to discipline a child is to yell. The average child under the age of eleven thinks concretely rather than in abstract terms. The way to discipline is not with screaming or nagging, although verbal reproof along with spanking is a biblical discipline technique.

Below are some procedures to follow in order to carry out the principles in the Word of God for raising and disciplining children.

Discipline should result from defiance of authority.

That word *defiance* is the key. A parent should not spank his child for making a mistake. The child should be reminded that parents make mistakes, too. Everybody makes mistakes. It is the defiance of authority that warrants discipline. When a child is instructed to do something and he understands the rules and goes against them to test parental authority, that is when a spanking is due.

Spanking should be immediate.

In Ecclesiastes 8:11, Solomon wrote: "Because sentence against an evil work is not executed speedily, therefore the heart of the sons of men is fully set in them to do evil." It is generally acknowledged that delayed trials and prosecution contribute to an increased crime rate. In similar fashion, delayed punishments for open rebellion by children are not very effective. For a mother to say, "I'm going to tell Dad when he gets home from work tonight, and you are really going to get it," is more harmful than beneficial. Not only will the delayed discipline be relatively ineffective, but also frequent messages of this sort will alienate the child from his father. The parent who sees the defiance should spank the child immediately.

Spanking should be done in private.

The parent must protect the child's sense of self-worth. If a parent spanks his child in the presence of other people, especially in the presence of other children, it diminishes his feelings of self-worth. He should be taken to a separate room and disciplined for his open rebellion privately.

Discipline can involve confession of guilt.

A parent may ask the disobedient child, "What did you do?" The parent should not ask the child *why* he disobeyed, because this will only teach him to justify his bad behavior. Ask him what he did that defied authority. He may say, "You know what I did." (Yes, you know what he did, but he should admit it.) He should not be forced to say he is sorry, because this may be teaching him to tell lies. He may not be sorry, but he *will* learn that he will suffer consequences for open defiance whether he is sorry or not.

Genuine parental grief is a useful discipline technique.

A loving parent will be genuinely sad when his child defies authority. The parent should not hide that grief, but rather should truthfully (not manipulatively) verbalize his sadness to the child. This will often bring about healthy feelings of true guilt in the child and genuine repentance on his part. This works especially well with older children and teenagers. It indirectly teaches the child that God responds with genuine grief to our sins, because He loves us and knows that our sins hurt ourselves in the end and prevent us from experiencing the abundant life God desires for us.

The consequences for the offense should be reasonable discipline.

Spanking should not be overdone. Many religious fanatics abuse their children "in the name of the Lord," through excessive spanking or beating the child with fists. Child abuse is a terrible parental sin. It is because of child

abuse cases that many well-intentioned individuals want
to outlaw physical punishment of children altogether. But
that would be an unwise overreaction. Sweden has out-
lawed spanking, and for several years now Sweden has
had the world's highest teenage suicide rate. Children need
limits to feel secure. For young children, we believe a
quick spank on the rear with a paddle or with the hand,
soon after the open defiance, is an excellent discipline
technique. For a defiant three year old, a slap on the back
of the hand may be all that is needed. For older children,
we believe other discipline techniques work better.

Discipline should involve reassurance and acceptance, without apology.

A parent should never say, "I'm sorry I spanked you."
He should not be sorry, since he is doing the will of God.
But he does need to reassure the child of his love. The
parent must make it clear that he is not casting the child
out or turning his back on the child. He is focusing on the
problem, not the child. He loves the child. So he asks,
"Why did I spank you?" The child should be encouraged
to tell his parent why he thinks he got the spanking. If the
child can admit, "I got a spanking because I stole Mary's
doll and ripped it up," then the discipline will be more
effective.

"Okay, that is why you got the spanking. That was
wrong, wasn't it?"

"Yes."

"And you are sorry, right?"

"Yes, I'm sorry." If he doesn't admit to being sorry, then
drop it. Don't make him lie by saying he is sorry if he

isn't. Either way, the parent should hug him and tell him he is loved.

Discipline may require restitution.

If the child has destroyed another child's property (or parent's property), he should replace it. The parent may have him use savings, give him special chores to do, or replace the broken toy with one of his own toys. This will teach him responsibility, and will also help to relieve his guilt.

Avoiding Breaking the Child's Spirit

While the concerned parent does what he can in a healthy way to quiet the young child's will, he must at the same time avoid breaking the child's spirit. Mature, healthy children grow up to be independent. They have many of their own likes and dislikes. They feel free to be creative and look at both sides of many issues. They are not all stamped in the same, rigid mold. Many parents wonder how they can discipline their children and yet allow them to develop their individuality. No parents are perfect—they all make mistakes. For children to turn out well-disciplined, obedient to authority, moral, and at the same time creative, independent, and confident in their own problem-solving abilities requires almost a miracle!

Following are some guidelines that will help parents to avoid breaking the spirit of their children.

Avoid too much spanking too early.

We have known well-intentioned parents who spanked young babies for wiggling while their diapers were being changed. Some parents punish their children for lack of toilet training at only one or two years of age (even though the average age for neurological readiness for toilet training isn't until two-and-a-half to three years of age). We have known a number of well-intentioned parents who were so determined to break the will of their child that they left all the "no-no's"—expensive vases, flowers, and sometimes even potentially dangerous items—right where they were before baby came. These unfortunate crawling infants were continually getting their hands slapped for grabbing "no-no's." Such children will grow up more likely to be hostile, rigid, uncreative, and paranoid. They will be afraid to look at creative alternatives to their political, religious, or philosophical views in life. They will be narrow-minded followers of dogmatic authority figures.

It is very important to realize that God gives all babies a natural bent toward curiosity. Curiosity is a God-given blessing that helps the young infant to learn. The one-year-old infant has more neurological sensitivity at his mouth area than he does in his fingertips, so he crawls or walks from item to item, putting things to his mouth to see what they feel like and taste like. As he looks at it to perceive it visually, he may even shake it to see what it sounds like. He is learning; he is maturing.

This type of exploration should be encouraged, not discouraged. Parents should remove all "no-no's," and especially dangerous items, from the infant's reach. The leading cause of death in infancy is accidents, for curiosity leads infants to drink furniture polish, fall out of cribs, and the like. Such tragedies can be prevented. When the infant is old enough to crawl out of his crib, he should be moved to a little bed rather than spanked every time he tries to crawl out of the crib. There are some dangerous things, like electrical sockets and cords, that cannot be removed from the reach of crawling infants. A slap on the back of his hand for grabbing a few "no-no's" will not break his spirit—if he is allowed and even encouraged to explore the majority of items within his reach. We believe that spanking should be used *only* for open rebellion— when the child does something that he already knows is wrong. An exception to this would be to stop the child from doing something dangerous, like running toward a busy street or pulling out electrical cords.

Avoid suppressing the child's emotions.

When God created the human brain, he divided the thinking portion of the human brain into two major areas: the cerebral cortex, the seat of logical thought, and the limbic lobe, the seat of our emotions. The mature adult is able to integrate his emotional awareness with his logical thought patterns to make wise decisions. These decisions will be far superior to the decisions made by the overly emotional person or the purely "logical" person, who makes wrong decisions because he is not in touch with his true feelings. Caring parents will try to encourage the development of both logical thought and emotions in their children. Many parents have heard the terrible saying that "children should be seen and not heard," and mistook it for a Bible verse. Following that slogan will produce children with low self-concepts, suppressed emotions, and chronic depressions as adults. As adults they will carry around unnecessary emotional pain.

Christ was the perfect God-man. He was (and is) God in human flesh. And Christ had feelings—He wept at the burial site of His friend Lazarus; He wept when the people of Jerusalem failed to recognize Him as Messiah; He became angry at the money changers and chased them with a whip; He angrily called the scribes and Pharisees a "generation of snakes and vipers"; He felt deep love for His mother, Mary, and for John, His disciple; His love for you and me was so deep that He shed His blood on the cross to pay for our personal sins. Our God is an emotional God, and Christ is an emotional Savior—and we are to follow Christ's example.

If parents punish their children when they verbalize their feelings, those children will learn to lie to themselves about their true feelings and will have broken spirits as adults. They will grow up to be computer-like people; perfectionistic workaholics. They will have hampered relationships with their mates and children, and will make many unwise decisions because of their lack of insight into their true emotions. They will unknowingly harbor much anger and resentment and frequently fight off depression.

Parents should not only allow their children to verbalize their feelings, they should encourage them to do so—even when the children are angry at their parents. Young children should be taught how to say, "I'm mad at you, Daddy," or "I'm mad at you, Mommy," in a polite, tactful way. Their temper tantrums should result in a good spanking; hitting or kicking parents out of anger should also bring punishment. But the child should be encouraged to share his anger politely. He should also be encouraged to share his other emotions, such as love, sadness, fear, and so on.

Verbalizing emotions with parents helps the child gain control over his emotions and use them to his advantage in life, rather than rejecting the use of half the brain God created in him. Parents who listen to the child's thinking and feelings show him how important he is to them; that child will develop a healthy sense of self-worth. If parent and child communicate feelings during the formative years, the child will have no need to act out his feelings in his teenage years.

Avoid nagging.

The Bible commands parents not to provoke their children to wrath—and nagging is certainly one parental behavior that will provoke wrath again and again. If the child knows the rules of the home (including his own chores and responsibilities), then he should be punished, not nagged at, when he breaks those known rules. Parents should never call their children names (though it may be tempting at times). Parents should politely verbalize their own anger toward the child for his disobedience. They should tell their child that he did a bad thing when he broke a rule; but parents should not call their child a "bad boy" or a "bad girl."

Handling Teenagers

The Book of Proverbs is filled with instructions about parent-child relationships, with several verses applicable to the father-teenager relationship. We see this especially in Proverbs 23. Verse 15 says, "My son, if thine heart be wise, my heart shall rejoice, even mine." And verse 19 reads, "Hear thou, my son, and be wise, and guide thine heart in the way." Verse 22 says, "Hearken unto thy father that begat thee, and despise not thy mother when she is old." And verse 26 says, "My son, give me thine heart, and let thine eyes observe my ways."

Many teenagers today have a spiritual vacuum in their lives. They have not been faced with the claims of Jesus Christ, are not brought to church by their parents, and are not taught the Bible in the home. Many of them know there is something missing, but they have not heard how to trust Christ. The vacuum needs to be filled with a relationship to Christ, and they also need a strong, meaningful relationship with their parents.

Elementary school children tend to idealize their parents. By the time they become teenagers, many are discovering that their parents have faults. Since they are too insecure to see their own faults, these teenagers become very angry at their parents for being "hypocrites," "dogmatic," or "rejecting," not realizing that they are doing the same things their parents are. Open communication is a must or the truth may never be seen.

Communicating with Teens

One reason why keeping the communication lines with teenagers open is so important is that the teenager's allegiance (including fellowship and morals) shifts to some extent from parents to peers. Parents must therefore maintain communication throughout this period so that their influence will still be felt, and so they can carry out their parental responsibilities.

One of the primary reasons that teenagers from Christian families reject the Christian way of life is simply communication breakdown. Somewhere along the line, often without the knowledge of the parents, the real communicating line between parent and teen has been lost. When that happens, trouble lies ahead. What can parents do about it? Time must be made for communicating.

1. Family devotions is an excellent time for talking, and for letting the children participate. Let the teens, especially, lead in prayer. Read portions of the Bible and comment on them. To help keep teens from "clamming up" (which they begin to do around age thirteen), as part of the family devotions ask every person to share the most meaningful thing that happened in the past twenty-four hours. This can be anything—a blessing from the Lord, hurt feelings, something about the Bible, something about answered prayer, a problem at school—whatever is most significant to the individual. This way what is going on in the inside will come out; family members are talking and thus sharing.

One family required the family members who refused to talk (or just thought they didn't have anything to say), to put twenty-five cents in the "kitty." Finally, enough money had accumulated for the family to go out to eat at a very special place. Parents should, however, keep devotions short enough not to bore the teenagers.

2. Another time for talking is when Dad regularly spends time with each child. This could be a "date" with each child and Dad at least once a month (see p. 68). This

will allow one-to-one communication between parent and child.

3. Time should be set aside regularly (say, once a week) for the family to get together for a family time of talking. There should also be a casual, open spirit that allows for talking any time throughout the week. Making time for communication cannot be overemphasized.

What do you talk about? There are many subjects a family should discuss. Family standards should be established so the family can work together as a unit. Standards about what? Standards about the use of the phone. Standards about the use of the car. Standards about the selection of friends. The kind of friends teens choose is perhaps one of the most vital issues they face, for it involves their future. Our teenagers need to be taught the importance of proper friends and circles of fellowship.

Standards for dating should also be discussed: whom to date; a plan for permission to date; where to go on a date; when to be back home. Parents and teenagers should discuss kissing, limitations on bodily contact before marriage, and how to handle difficult situations. Parents should listen to the teenager's opinions on these various situations, asking, What would you do if this happened? What would you do if that happened? What would you say if somebody offered you this? What if somebody did this to you or that to you, what would you do? Prepare them. This is the responsibility of parents, and teens need to talk about these things.

Parents and teenagers should also discuss attitudes. There is no way to change attitudes without talking about them. Attitudes are non-verbal communication. They are often expressions of problems and conflicts within. Pouting and the "silent treatment" are non-verbal ways of expressing problems. Parents need to encourage their teens to transfer from the non-verbal to the verbal.

The attitude a teen develops toward his mother will affect the attitude he will have toward people in general, and especially women, the rest of his life. The attitude that a teenager has toward his father is the attitude that a teenager will generally have toward God and male authority figures the rest of his life.

Atheists are made, not born. Many atheists come from families where the father is gone most of the time, or if he is present, he is negativistic. Many agnostics believe that there is some kind of "god" or "life-force" or "something" out there in the distance, but not a loving, caring, personal God. In our counseling experience, most agnostics come from homes with a cold, passive father who is usually not home. The religious liberal tends to come from a home where the father is mushy, overly sweet, and gives no restrictions on behavior. The children do whatever they like to do, and they can have anything they want if the parents can afford it. They grow up expecting God to spoil them, too. They want something for nothing. So proper attitudes are important and should be a point of communication.

Discipline for Teens

Discipline for a teenager must be much more sophisticated than it is for a small child. As the child grows older, there is a point at which the physical-type of spanking must be tapered off and a different type of discipline adopted. Parents can now move from the physical to the mental, from the physical to the counseling-type or restrictive-type of discipline.

Some parents may reserve the option to use physical discipline if it is absolutely necessary, but if they haven't reared their children properly, this is almost a lost cause when they get to be teenagers. If the parent suddenly decides to start training his children when they are in their teen years, he has an almost impossible task ahead. The best way to develop good teens is to do a good job of parenting when they are little. Spanking in the older years becomes more of a source of resentment and anger rather than a learning process. The parent may restrict the teenager by spanking, or may be successful in holding him back from doing something, but he probably hasn't changed the teenager's attitude. He is still the same inside.

As teens grow up, parents have to begin treating them as they would treat adults. Parents must do much more reasoning with them, for they are becoming responsible people. Parents need to encourage them to use their own reasoning, their minds, and their emotions. Teens must begin to rely on their own discernment of Scriptures, their own understanding of biblical principles, and must realize their own responsibility to yield to the Lord, allowing Him to have His way in their lives.

When the parents do have to take some punitive, restrictive measures, there are three kinds of discipline: involving things, places, and people. For example, suppose a teen repeats a minor rebellion until there needs to be some type of discipline. Parents can start with some re-

strictions of *things*, such as the use of the phone, car, television, or the like. There are many things that make up
teens' lives that can be considered. Parents can make a
restriction related to the offense, such as losing car privileges for a few days if the teenager willfully breaks a
specific, agreed-upon rule for the use of the family car.

If the parent needs to go to another level, he can restrict
places. Parents can restrict the teenager from taking part
in some activity, from going to a football or baseball game,
from going to a friend's house. If the teenager breaks a
known dating rule, for example, he may benefit by losing
one or two dating nights so he can become more responsible next time. When parents practice restrictive measures with a teenager, however, they should rarely restrict
something that would be spiritually beneficial to the teen.

The last level is the restriction of *people*. Maybe a teen
will be restricted from seeing a certain friend for a week
or from dating a certain person for a week, depending on
the seriousness of the offense. The teenager should have
as much freedom as possible in choosing friends or dates,
but limits are sometimes an absolute necessity.

Family Democracy

It is extremely beneficial for teenagers to feel they have
a part in the family operations. Below is a plan many
families would find helpful, called *family democracy*. In
a family where everybody is serious about spiritual matters, this plan works very well, especially if there are teenagers in the home. It will help teens develop a sense of
self-worth, self-confidence, and responsibility.

1. Every member must be willing to submit to the majority vote of the family. If there is an agreement of every member to submit to the majority vote, the plan can work.

2. The father is the president and has veto power, but he should use that power only when he feels it is absolutely necessary. If he uses it too often, obviously, the whole idea of the democracy will fall apart. The father abides by the majority vote just like everybody else, but he is the head of the family according to the Scriptures. He does have veto power if it is an emergency situation. As president he can keep issues from being considered if the health, safety, and welfare of the family or any person is in danger.

3. Any member can call for a family council, and all members must be present for every council meeting. Anybody, including the littlest child, the teenager, mom or dad, can call for a family council. Everybody stops what he is doing and joins the group for an immediate session.

4. Any member can have the floor to express himself. This is very important to teenagers. When we counsel with teenagers they often tell us, "My parents won't listen to me. They are not interested in my point of view." Parents sometimes do put their teenagers down, feeling that they are too inexperienced to speak knowledgeably on a subject. But whether theirs is a good idea or not, teens still need to communicate. They need to have the floor and the freedom to give their point of view without interruption. If parents stifle them, they have cut off communication, and that is the very thing parents must *not* do. They must encourage communication.

5. Take a vote. This can be either an open vote or a secret ballot.

6. Any issue that affects the family or a member of the family is fair game. The wife should, of course, feel free to vote differently than her husband. Some possible issues are where to eat out, if the family cannot agree, or where to go for a vacation. What does the father do if everyone wants to go to Hawaii? Here is a great opportunity for the father to teach his teenagers some basic economics. He can set out what the family income is and what the bills are. He can let them see how the parents have set up the budget, how it operates, and what the priorities are. Then, after the children have learned this, they can decide whether a trip to Hawaii would be reasonable.

The family council can also decide on the rules of the home, and together they can write a family contract. Should Dad go to church with the family on Sundays? Call for a family council. If he is committed to it, he should obey the vote. Should Dad, or someone else in the family, get help for his or her problem? Maybe one of the parents is an alcoholic or someone else has a serious problem with temper. Maybe the teenager has started to hitch-hike (he says that everybody is doing it). Call for a family council. If family members have agreed to submit to the majority vote, they will each have to trust the family judgment. Indeed, a teenager will sometimes respond more quickly to the family council than to mom or dad. The TV schedule might also be a subject for a family council—there are many areas in which this idea of a family council can help promote communication.

7. Family devotions is a good time to call for a family council. This way the family democracy plan can revolve around the desire to make Jesus Christ the center of the home. One cannot have a Christian home without Christ. Parents can't hope to be successful with their children unless they are interested in spiritual things, in reading the Bible, in calling on the Lord in prayer, and in living the Word in their daily lives.

A preacher once led the funeral for a man he had never met. Before the service, he said to the teenage son, "I never had the privilege of meeting your dad. He must have been a nice man. Do you know if your father was a Christian?"

The boy replied, "I don't know. I never heard him pray."

How would you feel if your children someday said, "Well, I don't know if my dad or mom were Christians; I never heard them pray. I never heard them talk about Jesus. I never heard them say they had accepted Christ as their Savior. I never did see their interest in spiritual things. I never saw them read the Bible. I never saw them go to church faithfully. I never saw their concern for a non-Christian neighbor. I never saw them teach a Sunday school class. I never saw them counseling with people or helping other Christians. I never heard them invite people who needed encouragement or some help from the Bible over to the house. I just don't remember it." That would indeed be a sad commentary.

A parent's most rewarding investment is the positive steps he implements to make his home more in line with the Word of God. The house that withstands the storms of life is that house built on the *doing* of the Word.

Five

Consistency

Tom was an eleven-year-old criminal. He had been in trouble with the law a number of times for breaking and entering homes, shoplifting, and vandalism. His parents were both teachers at a Christian school.

Tom was the "baby" of the family. His father believed in strict discipline, but didn't show much love. His mother acted as though she loved her son immensely, but she was extremely lenient with the boy, letting him get his own way nearly all of the time. In reality, the mother demonstrated her own insecurity by craving the son's acceptance. She could not tolerate disciplining him because his temporary anger was too overwhelming to her. Whenever the boy's father (who showed his insecurity through his sternness and rigidity) threatened to discipline him, the boy would run to his mother for protection. By age eleven, the courts were requiring this boy to get long-term psychiatric care for his sociopathy. Tom was a product of inconsistency.

Some parents basically agree with each other about discipline in the home, but they are very inconsistent about it. When they are in a jovial mood, they may laugh at a child's rebellious behavior, thus rewarding him for it. But when they are in a bad mood, they may be overly strict and punish the child for legitimate mistakes that are not acts of open rebellion. This type of parental inconsistency is very damaging to the child's personality. A child needs to know his limits. It increases his security level and decreases his anxiety level. At least at a subconscious level, children want limits. One reason why children "act up" is to find out if the parents love him enough and consider him significant enough to set limits and enforce them consistently.

Children from overly strict homes, if the strictness is not extreme, still tend to turn out to be healthy, contributing adults if their parents were fairly consistent. Children from overly lenient homes, if the lenience is not extreme, also tend to turn out to be fine citizens as adults if their parents practiced the other factors listed in this book and were fairly consistent. But out of all the hundreds of criminal types we have counseled as psychiatrist or pastor, approximately two-thirds came from homes where at least one parent spoiled the child excessively, thus teaching him that he could always get whatever he wanted if he manipulated enough. One-third came from homes where at least one parent was physically abusive or severely verbally abusive. In nearly all the cases of sociopathy we have counseled, parental inconsistency was a major causative factor.

One main way to guarantee consistency in discipline is to use written family contracts. When the children are very young, a family contract may need revision only once every year or two. But during the teenage years, it may need revision every two or three months. A lengthy family council meeting is the best time to write up a family contract, and everyone in the family should participate in creating it. The parents could have the oldest child draw a line down the middle of a piece of paper, writing "Rules and Chores" at the top of the left column and "Consequences" at the top of the right column. (Consequences is a nice word for punishments). If the children are quite varied in their ages, separate contracts, or at least separate sections on the large family contract, will probably be necessary for each child. This is because the older and more mature a child gets, the more freedoms he should be trusted with—and also the more responsibilities (chores) he should have in the home. By the time he is a senior in high school, he should be trustworthy enough to have almost no rules and an adult share of the chores in the home.

Ask the children for their opinions on what the rules and chores ought to be, including rules for the parents (such as agreeing to go to church with the children, or agreeing not to nag, with a verbal apology as a parental 'consequence"). As the children make their suggestions, the family can vote on each one—with the father having veto power, of course.

When listing rules, chores, and consequences, it is extremely important to be very specific. For example, a child's chore should not be listed merely, "Carry out the gar-

bage." It should be spelled out more specifically, such as,
"Carry out the garbage every Monday and Thursday morning by 8:15 A.M." The consequence should also be specific,
and should (as much as possible) be related to the offense.
In other words, if the child forgets to take out the garbage
or purposely skips this chore, a good consequence would
be an extra, unpopular chore to complete before supper,
such as cleaning out the garage or a bathroom. But the
specific consequence should be spelled out on the contract
and voted on by the whole family.

This type of contract can eliminate nagging. When 8:14
A.M. rolls around, and the child has not yet carried out
the garbage, the parents should not remind him of his
chore or nag him about it. They should let him either
remember it by himself in the next sixty seconds, or suffer
the consequences of forgetting it. This will teach him responsibility. When he is an adult, his mother won't be
following him around on his job, reminding him of his
next duty!

If the family is in doubt about how strict or lenient to
be on certain rules, it might be a good idea to phone some
other sets of parents whose children seem well-adjusted,
and get their opinion on those questions. There are many
areas of discipline that God's Word does not address specifically, and parents must use their best judgment on
what is fair. Staying close to the average rules and chores
for Christian families with well-adjusted children in your
neighborhood will help prevent resentments in your children. If the rules and chores the children suggest are reasonable, then leave them as they are. If they are too lenient
or too strict, the father may need to modify them some-

what—but he should only do so with much consideration and careful listening to the views of the children and his wife. When the list is completed, both parents should sign it and date it. Then each child should sign it as well, thus agreeing to abide by it.

The children may break one or two of the rules in the next twenty-four hours. This is common, and usually represents a conscious or subconscious attempt on the part of the child to test his limits. He wants to find out if the parents care enough about him to take the effort to consistently enforce the contract. The contract is useless if the parents don't carefully carry out the consequences when they are called for. This does not mean the parents should be rigid and inflexible. There will be occasions when a chore needs to be swapped or put off, or when a teenager should under special circumstances be allowed to stay out an hour or two longer than his usual deadline on a date. But be consistent. Remember that the children don't exist for the rules. The rules, like the laws of our land, exist for the benefit of the individuals subject to those rules.

After a two- or three-month trial of the new contract, it is advisable for the family to have another council meeting to discuss how the contract is working out. Modifications may need to be made. A formerly rebellious child may be behaving much better, so increased freedom may be an appropriate reward. The opposite may also be true. If one of the children is consistently breaking the rules, narrowing his limits may be in order. Each child should be given as much freedom as his parents can trust him with. It is better for the child if the parents make a slight mistake by trusting him too much, rather than make the mistake of trusting him too little, because most children will try to live up to their parents' trust (or lack of trust).

One of the most important factors is, of course, to keep open the lines of communication between parent and child. We have suggested this contracts technique for many families we have counseled, and the families have nearly always felt that it helped eliminate many of the communication problems between the parents and the children. It also has helped ease the traditional parent-child power struggle, by acknowledging that the child is a significant person and by valuing his opinions on the rules he ought to have.

For cases of adolescent depression or adolescent rebellion, the family democracy plan is our standard approach, and it works most of the time. Interestingly, when it doesn't work, it is usually the fault of the parents, who are too lazy to consistently enforce the rules when the teenager tests them. Some parents come to our offices expecting us (as pastor or psychiatrist) to be able to wave some magic wand over their rebellious child and somehow "cure" him. These parents don't expect us to tell them there are things *they* can do to help "cure" these conflicts. As Abraham Lincoln once said, "Most people are about as happy as they choose to be."[1]

Husband and wives *must* provide a united front. If par-

1. For further information on how to resolve depression in people of all ages, we would refer you to a book that Dr. Paul Meier coauthored with his medical partner, Dr. Frank Minirth, entitled *Happiness Is a Choice* (Baker, 1978).

ents disagree on discipline, they should not do so in front of the children. Even before the family council meets to work out a contract, it would be good for the parents to meet privately and reach some personal compromises. On non-discipline issues, it is actually beneficial for the children to observe the parents disagreeing in front of them, then discussing the disagreement and resolving the difference. It models problem-solving for the children, and will make divorce less likely when the children grow up and have problems of their own to resolve.

On matters of discipline, however, it is better for the parents to resolve these privately, or else the children will try to manipulate one parent against the other. If the husband and wife are unable to reach a compromise, they must remember that God has established the husband as the leader in the home, so his decision must ultimately stand. Even if he is too strict, the children will live through it—consistency is the most important factor. If things start to backfire on him, he may decide to change his mind on his own. Mark Twain once said, "All women, and some great men, change their minds."

In his book, *Man in Transition*, Gary Collins notes that children need to feel accepted by their parents in order to accept themselves. Dr. Collins states,

> Jesus accepted everyone—even the unlovely—although He didn't always accept their behavior. Christian parents and church members must do the same. This acceptance by others, however, should be consistent. It is hard for a child to feel accepted if he gets favorable treatment at one time and unfavorable treatment at other times. Even when chil-

dren are being disciplined, parents can show that they accept and love the child, in spite of his undesirable behavior.[2]

King David once wrote, "LORD, who shall abide in thy tabernacle? who shall dwell in thy holy hill?" (Ps. 15:1). David answered that if we want to abide in God's tabernacle, that is, have fellowship with God, we must be consistent even if it sometimes hurts. David said that God honors "them that fear the LORD. He that sweareth to his own hurt, and changeth not" (Ps. 15:4). In the New Testament, Peter instructs us, "Finally, be ye all of one mind, having compassion one of another, love as brethren, be pitiful, be courteous: Not rendering evil for evil, or railing for railing: but contrariwise blessing; knowing that ye are thereunto called, that ye should inherit a blessing" (I Peter 3:8-9). We would encourage Christian parents to follow Peter's advice and apply it to their child-rearing practices by being compassionate, courteous, and "of one mind," consistent with each other and with their children.

2. Gary R. Collins, *Man in Transition: The Psychology of Human Development* (Carol Stream, Ill.: Creation House, 1971).

Six

Setting the Example

Children learn behavior patterns much more by what they see their parents doing than by what they hear their parents saying. Parents could read this book several times, have family council meetings, write excellent family contracts, and still have depressed and rebellious children, if they do not set a reasonable example. Of course, no parents are perfect—we all make mistakes every day. But some parents don't seem to realize how contradictory their words and actions are.

Jack M. was a forty-five-year-old father who was being treated in our psychiatry ward for alcoholism. During a group therapy session, Mr. M. avoided discussing his own problems by bragging to the group about what a good disciplinarian he was with his children. He told us that he made his children go to church every Sunday morning, Sunday night, and Wednesday night. When a group member asked him if he went with them, he replied, "Well, no, I don't, because I'm too restless and can't sit still that long." Then he bragged about how he made his children study their school work for one hour every night and also read their Bible every night. I asked him if he studied very much or read his Bible every day. He replied, "Well, no, I don't, because I get bored too easy when I read." Mr. M. still went on to brag that he didn't let his children watch any television whatsoever. When a group member asked him why, he replied, "Because there's too many beer commercials on TV." I asked him what he had been doing every night for the past few years, and he finally admitted, "I've been sitting at home watching television every night and drinking about a fifth of whiskey every night." He was offended that we made him aware of the fact that he was setting a poor example for his children. His children will probably turn out the very opposite of what he wants, because he is telling them one thing and practicing another.

When parents are working on a family contract during counseling sessions, we discourage parents from making any rule for the children that they don't practice themselves (within reason). For example, parents who smoke should not have a no smoking rule. Parents who regularly abuse prescription drugs should not have rules against drugs for their children. Parents who use foul language should not have a foul language rule for their children. And parents who do not attend church regularly should also make church optional for their children. There are, of course, some privileges parents should have that are related to marital status, age, and position within the family.

On a positive note, there are many ways that parents can carry out the duty of setting the example:

Serving Christ in a healthy local church

It will make a tremendous impact on children's lives if they grow up observing their parents using their God-given talents and gifts to teach Sunday school, sing in the choir, perform the duties of a deacon, socialize with newcomers, help other Christians and non-Christians in times of need, or pray for the needs of others. It is equally important that Christian parents do not get overly involved in any local church to the detriment of their children.

If a child needs attention from his parents, but they are too busy supposedly "serving God" to meet his needs, he will probably subconsciously blame God for his parents' self-righteous form of ungodliness and as an adult reject God for taking his parents away from him as a child. Pastors should encourage each parent to find one avenue of service that he or she can do well, then discourage that overly eager parent from getting involved in more than one or two kinds of service. A parent can find his most suitable area of service by asking himself the following four questions: What do I like to do that promotes the cause of Christ? What do my friends think I'm good at in helping the cause of Christ? What talents have I used that have benefited others? What is the Holy Spirit giving me a desire to do, and how can I know that it really is the Holy Spirit and not some hidden human motivation within me?

Establishing healthy priorities

Each person's priorities are an individual matter between him and God—we have no right to dictate to anyone what they should be specifically. However, based on our knowledge of God's Word and on our counseling experiences, here is a priority list we would suggest that every reader consider:

1. Spend a little time each day getting to know God better.
2. Take care of one's own mental health (recreation, reflection, rest, etc.).
3. Spend some time nearly every day meeting the needs of one's mate—especially communication needs.
4. Spend at least an hour or two nearly every day meeting the needs of one's children, including playing with them and listening to them. This applies to fathers just as much as mothers.
5. Spend some time each week serving Christ in a way that will not take time away from priorities 1, 2, 3, or 4.
6. Find a job that will provide for the family's needs but will not take time away from priorities 1, 2, 3, 4, or 5.

Meeting one's own needs, and modeling this for children

Some people feel guilty for taking care of their own needs, not realizing that when one meets his own physical, emotional, and spiritual needs he will be able to be a happier and better mate, parent, and Christian. No human ever had perfect parents—all humans carry around a few scars and unmet needs from early childhood. Some didn't get enough "fathering." Some didn't get enough "mothering." Others didn't get enough "brothering" and "sistering." Some never received much praise for worthwhile things they did. Some never received much forgiveness for past mistakes. Some have never forgiven themselves.

The local church does not exist merely for teaching non-Christians how to accept Christ. Evangelism is an important function of the church, but a healthy church will also meet the spiritual and emotional needs of its members, all of whom are needy humans with personal needs. The local church can provide "fathering," "mothering," "brothering," and "sistering" in a way that makes up for deficiencies of childhood. Good Bible teaching can also help build spiritual strength and give guidelines for practical Christian living.

Suppose a child senses that his mother feels lonely. If he hears her humbly verbalizing that lonely feeling, then sees her responsibly taking care of that feeling by getting together with a friend for some fellowship, he learns a great deal about dealing with needs. An unhealthy, dependent person goes through life with unmet needs and blames the world around him for not meeting those needs. A healthy person goes through life using God's power in his life to meet his own needs responsibly. He humbly admits these needs to others, and humbly accepts the help of others—while gladly returning their love. A healthy person realizes his own parents were not perfect, stops expecting them to somehow "come through" to meet his childhood needs for, say, unconditional acceptance. The healthy person forgives his imperfect parents for the mistakes they have made and appreciates the things his parents did right. The unhealthy person keeps trying fruitlessly to gain the unconditional acceptance of his parents, naively assuming that his parents will some day "come through."

When a child sees that his parents have physical, emotional, or spiritual needs, and he hears them admit this, it helps the child realize he is not the only one who has "hurts" sometimes. When he sees his parents pray about their needs, he learns to pray and seek God's guidance for his own needs. When he sees his parents meet their needs, and enjoy "the abundant life" that God intended, the child learns problem-solving techniques himself. He is in the process of becoming a well-adjusted, responsible adult.

God said, "O that there were such an heart in them, that they would fear me, and keep all my commandments always, that it might be well with them, and with their children forever!" (Deut. 5:29). Here God shows His tremendous love for us by expressing His desire that we live by His principles. He wants things to go well not only for us, but also for our children and our children's children. He is saying that if we set good examples, generations after us will benefit. Do you want your children to exhibit the fruit of the Spirit? Then practice "love, joy, peace, patience, kindness, goodness, faithfulness, gentleness, self-control" (Gal. 5:22-23, NASB). Do you want your children to be truthful? Then follow God's instruction when He tells us to speak the truth in love (see Eph. 4:15). Do you want your children to forgive each other, and to forgive you for mistakes you have made? Then follow God's instruction when He tells you, "And be ye kind one to another, tenderhearted, forgiving one another, even as God for Christ's sake hath forgiven you" (Eph. 4:32).

Any overseer in a local church has an added God-given responsibility for "setting the example." God strongly warns Christians that any overseer must be "one that ruleth well his own house, having his children in subjection with all gravity; (For if a man know not how to rule his own house, how shall he take care of the church of God?) (I Tim. 3:4-5). God's Word is quite blunt here. If a man is not managing his own family well, he is setting a bad example and has no right to try to manage God's flock. Anyone who does so in spite of this warning is acting contrary to the written will of God. This does not mean a pastor or deacon should have perfect children—only that he should be a good manager whose children are under his subjection. We have tremendous respect for deacons we have known who have requested a one- or two-year "time out" from the deacons' board to get some counseling and get their own family's needs taken care of. That is a better example than almost anything else a man in that situation could do, and will help other leaders in the church to reconsider their own example-setting priorities.

Seven

Proper Leadership Roles

Marriage was invented by God. The first marriage ceremony was performed by God. God gave marriage to man as the first institution, even before He gave man the church. Marriage is more important than the church. In fact, the church is built on strong building blocks called homes: we must not take marriage lightly. Cohabitation without marriage is not a biblical option.

There are many marriages in which neither partner is interested in making any changes. They have their minds set on getting their own ways, and refuse to acknowledge some things that may be wrong. In this case, all a counselor can do is pray. But this book is for those who are interested in making their marriages work.

The Role of the Husband

In I Timothy 3:2-5, the Lord, through the apostle Paul, describes the qualifications a pastor must have. Later, he repeats nearly the same qualifications for a deacon, and these are applicable to any man of spiritual maturity. These qualifications should be studied very carefully by those desiring to learn God's will for the role of a husband or father over his family. These qualities should be goals for any husband and father who is a growing Christian.

> A bishop then must be blameless, the husband of one wife, vigilant, sober, of good behaviour, given to hospitality, apt to teach; Not given to wine, no striker, not greedy of filthy lucre; but patient, not a brawler, not coveteous; One that ruleth well his own house, having his children in subjection with all gravity; (For if a man know not how to rule his own house, how shall he take care of the church of God?) (I Tim. 3:2-5).

The first responsibility of the bishop-husband in this passage, as far as his role in the home is concerned, is that of leader of his house. The words *ruleth* in verse 4 and *rule* in verse 5 come from the Greek word which means "to stand before, to lead or attend to."[1] If somebody is a leader of a store or a large corporation, or is the president of a club or of a class, he is to *manage* that entity. The Scripture says that one who is to be responsible for leading a church must have proved that he can manage his own house.

There are several things a leader does. First, he manages that over which he has the responsibility. In the home, there should be nothing that goes on without the husband's awareness or approval.

1. W. E. Vine, *An Expository Dictionary of New Testament Words* (Old Tappan, N.J.: Revell, 1966), p. 307.

Second, in his role as the husband, a leader delegates responsibility. A manager does not do everything himself; he has learned to utilize the gifts and abilities of other people. He needs to recognize the gifts and abilities of his wife and utilize her gifts in the operation of the home.

In the Old Testament Book of Proverbs we see a good example of this in the well-known chapter about the virtuous woman. Proverbs 31:10 says, "Who can find a virtuous woman? for her price is far above rubies." The word virtuous means "a force with deep reserves."[2] It carries the idea of a complex, resourceful woman with many gifts and abilities. The beautiful thing about the description in this passage is that it appears that the woman's husband has delegated to her many responsibilities according to her gifts. This makes him a good manager. He has recognized her abilities, and he has given her liberty and responsibility to exercise those gifts.

For instance, look at verse 16: "She considereth a field, and buyeth it." Her husband, knowing her gifts, has given her the responsibility of several businesses on the side. He has given her the responsibility of looking over the real estate, considering it, and buying it if she thinks it is worth buying. Not only that, but in the last part of verse 16, we see that she oversees a vineyard. She has people working for her, and no doubt has the gift of administration. Notice in verse 24: "She maketh fine linen, and selleth it." She is in the linen business, besides all the responsibilities in her house. The Bible does not say that a woman should

2. Strong's Concordance.

not work outside her house. But it does imply that a woman must take care of the responsibilities in her house first.

The godly man utilizes his wife's gifts and abilities in certain areas to make a complete team effort to operate that home. If the wife, for instance, is better at math than the husband, there is no reason why the responsibility of paying the bills and keeping the checking accounts in order should not be delegated to her. Some husbands feel that their leadership is somehow diminished if they do not assume all the responsibilities in the home. If they give any kind of responsibility to the wife, they feel they are not being a man. This is, of course, not true. It does not mean he is relinquishing his masculinity; he is not backing away from his responsibilities. In fact, he is exercising that responsibility properly.

There are many other areas. Each husband should think about the wife that God has given him and consider her abilities. Then he should be careful not to hinder her from operating in those areas where God has enabled her to excel. This attitude will bless the home.

The marriage tests we use include the question: "Husbands, do you understand your role in the home?" A second question is: "Have you defined your role to your wife? Does she know what her role is? Have you taken time to communicate and tell her what you expect of her?" Many of our clients answer both questions, "no." Our experience shows that often couples go into marriage with assumptions that are unscriptural, which they have usually learned from their own families as they grew up. They have differing ideas and clashing philosophies that cause communication breakdown. The partners do not come to the Word of God and submit to it, and the result is trouble.

Scripture teaches that the husband is the head of the wife. The apostle Paul gave us a beautiful illustration of how this is to work in marriage: "For the husband is the head of the wife, even as Christ is the head of the church: and he is the saviour of the body" (Eph. 5:23). We conclude by looking at this comparison that the husband is the final "authority"[3] in the home, as Christ is the final authority over the church. He is our Lord. We don't all vote and then tell Him what to do. He is our Master; He is the head of the body. But again, because we are the body of which He is the head, we have a function in the operation of the church. The Lord has given each Christian certain gifts and talents to use for Him. While our head, Jesus Christ, is at the Father's right hand in heaven, He expects us to express and operate those gifts God has given to us with joy and with purpose. Therefore, if a man is to take his position as head over his wife, as Christ is head of the church, he has the option of final decision-making in the home, but in so doing he must recognize and use his wife's gifts in a spirit of love and purpose.

Verse 25 tells us that this leadership is bathed in love, just as Christ's leadership to His church. "Husbands, love your wives, even as Christ also loved the church, and gave himself for it." When the husband makes decisions as head of the house, his decisions should be based on love for his wife and his children. If a husband makes decisions purely on the basis of his own interests, he is not fulfilling

3. Vine, *New Testament Words*, p. 202.

his role as a leader with love. But if the husband follows the biblical guidelines, then he considers the needs of his wife, the needs of his children, and the needs of his home. His decisions are based on a loving desire to meet their needs. He ought to love his wife enough to die for her, as we read in verse 25.

If the husband is willing to die for his wife, she should be willing to live for him. Jesus was willing to die for the church—that is, for sinners who became His church. As a result, the Bible tells us, we should be willing to live for Him out of gratitude. That is the way it works. Husbands should love their wives as Christ loves the church. They should love their wives so that they *know* that they are loved.

Verse 29 says, "For no man ever yet hated his own flesh; but nourisheth and cherisheth it." Paul is talking about Christ's relationship to the church, and to the man nourishing and cherishing his wife. These are key words. If a man is to be the right kind of leader, he will lead with *love*. This means he accepts the responsibility of provision and security in several areas. He nourishes and cares for his wife. He is responsible for her physical security.

He should also nourish and care for her *spiritually*. He will lead the way concerning church, family altar, prayer, and will seek to give counsel and guidance when needed. A good husband is also interested in nourishing and caring for his wife mentally and emotionally. He will see that she is intellectually challenged and encouraged to share her true emotions as well. She should never be afraid to tell him how she feels.

The Role of the Wife

Ephesians 5:22 reads, "Wives, submit yourselves unto your own husbands, as unto the Lord." And verse 24 says, "Therefore as the church is subject unto Christ, so let the wives be to their own husbands in every thing." The word *submit* identifies one of the aspects of the role of a Christian wife. She is to submit to her husband's management. The Greek word translated *submit* means "to rank under, to be under obedience."[4]

Actually, this is true freedom for the wife. In God's world there is no such thing as freedom without a structured relationship. A derailed train is not free; it is free to make progress only if it is on the right track.

God knows how He created us; God knows the purpose for our lives; God knows what freedom truly is. Wives find real freedom when they place themselves within the restriction of and submission to the management of their loving husbands. That does *not* mean a wife is not allowed to communicate. It does *not* mean that she cannot share her feelings. It certainly does not carry the idea that a woman is to be the slave, with the man cracking a whip around the house. Of course not. In fact, the apostle Peter talks about a wife living with a non-Christian husband (I Peter 3). She is admonished to submit to him, to obey him, and follow him, but she is not to be afraid. She is not to fear expressing herself. In her role as a submitted partner under the leadership of the leader of the house, she is always to have the freedom to express herself on any issue,

4. Ibid., pp. 76-77.

even if it is a controversial issue. There should always be a way to sit down and talk in cool, calm voices, sharing ideas.

But how far should a wife obey her husband?

Mary Jane was perplexed about her home situation. Her husband, Bill, had told her that she had to go to an X-rated movie with him that evening, whether she liked it or not.

If she is a Christian wife, what should she do? What would you tell her to do? Doesn't the Bible say she is to submit to the management of her husband? First of all, when a woman's husband asks her to do something which would violate her convictions, she needs to try to discern what his real goal is. Mary Jane should try to discover what her husband is actually saying. Is his message, "You are going to go with me because I want you to be with me"? Getting to know Bill better would help a counselor to figure out Bill's motives. Perhaps she is sexually frigid and has not sought counseling to get over her frigidity. Or perhaps he wants her to sin as much as he does so he won't feel as guilty.

Mary Jane needs to politely express to Bill her analysis of his goal. She could respond, "Dear, are you really trying to say that I have not been willing to spend enough time with you? Is that why you want me to go with you, to be with you more, to spend more time together? Or is it because of my sexual problem, or your guilt problem?" Bill might say, "Well, actually I am angry at you for being so frigid at times. It's a real put-down to me. I thought taking you to an X-rated movie might loosen you up a bit." Then Mary Jane could devise an alternative for reaching her husband's goal without violating her convictions. She could say, "Bill, you are absolutely right. I have put off working on my sexual conflicts long enough. But going to an X-rated movie would only make matters worse for me. Would you be willing instead to go with me to see a Christian psychiatrist to work on this problem together?"

If Bill refuses, she could then ask for permission to go for counseling by herself. Since resolving her sexual conflicts would benefit Bill, he would almost certainly allow this creative alternative. If Bill is so obnoxious that he still insists that she violate her conscience by going to the X-rated movie, and she is certain that going to an X-rated movie would displease God, then she should refuse to disobey God in this situation and politely refuse to go with him.

In Genesis 2:18, the role of the wife is described as one who is a *suitable helper*: "It is not good that the man should be alone; I will make him an help meet for him." The noun *help* in this verse means "helper, assistant." The wife's role is to be an assistant, a helper. The word *meet* means "suitable." Timothy says "meet [suitable] for the master's use." According to the Scriptures, then, the wife is to be a suitable helper, a suitable assistant to her husband.

We already noticed in Proverbs 31 that this woman was given the responsibility of running several businesses on the side. But notice that before anything else is mentioned, she is said in verse 12 to be a suitable helper. She is a woman who is oriented to her husband: "She will do him good and not evil all the days of her life."

There are many Christian homes that are child-oriented, and that is wrong. There are many husbands who are job-oriented; they are headed for trouble. Within the marriage realm, the husband is to be wife-oriented and the wife is to be husband-oriented, and together they are to be God-oriented and Bible-oriented.

Since the wife is to be a helper suitable to her husband, she complements every part of his life. The wife often makes up for the deficiencies in his personality and in his approaches to things (and vice versa). The husband may express ideas, but because of prejudices in our culture, he may deny his feelings. The wife may then be very good at being in touch with and verbalizing feelings. He may desire success in business to prove himself. She may primarily desire financial and emotional security. Together they may strike a better balance. He may be more pragmatic and practical, and she may be more impulsive (or vice versa). Again, they are stronger together than they are apart. This shows how God has designed the wife for the husband and the husband for the wife.

The wife helps in the decision-making process. That is why it is important for a husband and wife to have regular times of communication, just to sit down and talk about anything—talk about feelings, talk about what is going on, laugh a little, joke a little, fellowship, express things, pray together.

There are six areas in marriage in which there should be full communication: (1) Money—make sure you are traveling the same road, for the majority of arguments in American marriages involve money; (2) sex; (3) spiritual things; (4) in-laws; (5) children; and (6) personality conflicts. The root problems, of course, run much deeper than these surface issues. But if one can keep the communication lines open, one can have a very good marriage.

When the husband and wife come to an impasse and they won't agree, they should temporarily drop the issue, and allow time for more facts on the situation to emerge. But if an emergency decision must be made, and if they cannot put it off, and they still don't see eye to eye, then obviously somebody has to give in. In this case the wife should submit to the husband. Marriages that don't follow this principle go bankrupt emotionally and spiritually.

Lastly, in the role of a woman the Bible tells us that she is to be responsible for the home and for the children. Titus 2:5 says that women are to be "discreet, chaste, keepers at home." We sometimes mistranslate that. It doesn't mean she must "keep herself at home," although that is not wrong. It means she is to be a keeper of the home. The word *homemaker* means one who is primarily responsible for the daily functions of the home. This does *not* mean that the husband shouldn't help or offer his assistance. Remember, he is the leader. If a leader sees that someone is bogged down in his work, he finds a way to help. He spots problems and comes up with solutions. However, the primary person responsible for keeping that home is the woman.

What if a wife works outside the home? If outside employment gets in the way of her responsibility at home, then she should quit her job, for the wife's first job is her home. Included in that description is responsibility for the children—seeing that they are fed and clothed properly, that they get enough rest, security, and love. This is primarily the wife's responsibility. When the husband is home, he is to help. He is to be the one to discipline if he is at home. But the job of the home is primarily the woman's. Proverbs 31:13 says she "worketh willingly with her hands." She does her work at home with delight.

A wife may say, "I hate this drudgery. I wish I had an outside job instead of the responsibility of marriage." But the virtuous woman does her job as a glory to God. She does it with delight. Proverbs 31:27 says, "She looketh well to the ways of her household . . ."—(It is *her* household; it is *her* responsibility)—". . . and eateth not the bread of idleness." Verse 15 says, "She riseth also while it is yet night, and giveth meat to her household." She prepares the meals. She doesn't sleep in and make her husband fix his own breakfast. This virtuous woman gets up while it is still night and gives food to her household. Perhaps housewives today who find themselves bored and un-challenged could follow the example of the ideal woman in Proverbs 31. Perhaps they could find some worthwhile part-time activity outside of the home, such as continuing education, or making some investments, or volunteer work at a hospital, or starting a home Bible-study. There are hosts of options, as long as the children and husband do not suffer.

Paul Meier is a Christian physician and psychiatrist with the Minirth Meier New Life Clinic in Richardson, Texas. He has conducted seminars throughout the United States on counseling and child-rearing.

Richard Meier is a licensed professional counselor and a licensed marriage and family therapist with the Minirth Meier New Life Clinic in Richardson, Texas. Before becoming a counselor, he served as a pastor for twenty-three years. He received his Th.M. from Clarksville School of Theology in Tennessee, his D.Min. from Trinity Thoological Seminary in Indiana, and a master's degree in counseling from Liberty University.